INTRODUCTION TO CSS FOR PAGED MEDIA

A Data Usability Company
ANTENNA HOUSE

INTRODUCTION TO
CSS
FOR PAGED MEDIA

Antenna House, Inc.

AH Formatter
V6.6

1 Paged Media   19 PDF

4 Headers & Footers   12 Characters   13 Counters

1

Introduction to CSS for Paged Media

7 Paragraphs   5 Columns   6 Keeps & Breaks

© 2019 Antenna House, Inc.[1]
© 2019 アンテナハウス株式会社

9 Tables   13 Japanese

While every precaution has been taken in the preparation of this document, the publisher assumes no responsibility for errors or omissions, or for damages resulting from the use of information contained herein.

11 Lists

Edition	Date
XML Prague 2019	February 7, 2019
Fifth Edition	November 9, 2018
Fourth Edition	April 3, 2018
Third Edition	April 21, 2009
Second Edition	March 13, 2009
First Edition	December 8, 2008

Antenna House, Inc.
500 Creek View Road
Suite 107
Newark, DE 19711
USA
Telephone +1 302-427-2456
sales@antennahouse.com
http://www.antennahouse.com/

15 Images   10 MathML & SVG

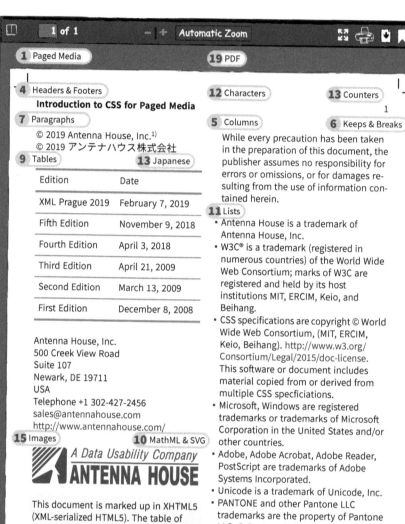

A Data Usability Company
ANTENNA HOUSE

This document is marked up in XHTML5 (XML-serialized HTML5). The table of contents, index, and syntax highlighting are updated using XSLT. Styles are specified using a CSS style sheet. The XHTML5, CSS, and image files are available on the Antenna House website. This document was formatted and converted to PDF with AH Formatter V6.6.

3 Background   2 Box Layout

8 Footnotes & Sidenotes   12 Colors   14 Cross-references

3 Page Layout

BRIEF CONTENTS

CONTENTS

INTRODUCTION

CSS is widely used in browsers, editors, and other applications. CSS is used not only for web design but also as the style sheet specification for a wide range of printing applications as well as for electronic paged media delivered as PDF.

CSS (Cascading Style Sheets) Level 1 became a W3C Recommendation in 1996. CSS 2 became a W3C Recommendation in 1998, and CSS 2.1 (Cascading Style Sheets Level 2 Revision 1), in 2011. At the time of writing, CSS 2.2 is under development.

CSS post-Level 2 is popularly known as CSS 3, but there will not be a single, monolithic CSS Level 3 specification. CSS beyond CSS Level 2 has been broken into multiple modules that define separate parts of CSS. These modules are numbered individually. The first versions of modules that build on CSS Level 2 are denoted as Level 3, and each may be superseded by a Level 4 version. For example, CSS Color Level 3 replaces several sections of CSS Level 2, and CSS Color Level 4, which is currently in development, will eventually replace CSS Color Level 3. Modules that do not build on CSS Level 2 features start at Level 1: for example, CSS Multi-Column Layout Level 1. CSS as a whole will still be referred to as CSS Level 3 even when some individual modules are at Level 4 and beyond.

Individual modules are in varying stages of development and varying levels of stability. The stability levels for all W3C specifications range from 'First Public Working Draft' to Recommendation'. The CSS Working Group maintains a separate stability categorization for its specifications that ranges from 'Rewriting' and 'Exploring' through to 'Stable' and 'Completed'.

The CSS Working Group compiles yearly snapshots of the current state of CSS at that point in time. CSS Snapshot 2017 lists both Recommendation and Candidate Recommendation specifications as comprising the official definition of CSS as of 2017.

CSS 2.1 (and CSS 2.2) provides only minimal support for paged media output, and its page layout features are not powerful enough. CSS 3, although still under development by the W3C, defines many of the features that are necessary for professional quality formatting, including: advanced page layouts; multiple columns; vertical writing; hyphenation; and multilingual character layout. Antenna House Formatter provides additional features for optimal formatting, including: custom-developed MathML 3, CGM, and SVG rendering; baseline grids; PANTONE® spot colors; and additional properties for controlling Japanese layout.

Using CSS in paged media design for XML and HTML is not yet common but its use is expected to increase as the development of CSS 3 progresses. *Introduction to CSS for Paged Media* aims to make CSS for Paged Media easy to understand.

Antenna House Formatter and CSS

The Antenna House Formatter family is available in multiple variants with different capabilities. Of these, Antenna House CSS Formatter can format either XML or HTML using CSS, and Antenna House Formatter can both format documents using CSS and format XSL-FO. Both of those are available as a Lite variant with reduced functionality. The standalone Windows GUI versions of these offer on-screen preview of formatted documents. Please see the Antenna House website for more information.

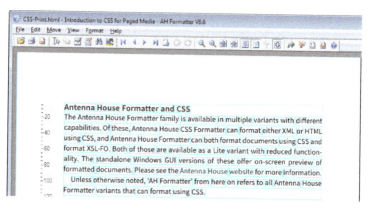

Antenna House Formatter GUI (with area borders and ruler shown)

Unless otherwise noted, 'AH Formatter' from here on refers to all Antenna House Formatter variants that can format using CSS.

Audience

Many people are familiar with CSS in the browser: some are very familiar, but others, not so much. Fewer people, however, are as familiar with using CSS for paged media.

Introduction to CSS for Paged Media is intended for you if you know CSS but have never written CSS for paged media. You should already have some familiarity with CSS syntax and with using common properties such as 'border', 'padding', 'font-size', and so on. This document does cover these, but not in great detail.

If you are fully familiar with most aspects of CSS but not with paged media, then these chapters will be the most useful to you: 3. PAGE LAYOUT; 4. HEADERS & FOOTERS; 17. COLOR; 14. IMAGE POSITIONING; and 19. PDF OUTPUT.

Since this is just an introduction to CSS for paged media, it does not attempt to cover every property, selector, rule, or function of either CSS or of AH Formatter. For more information on the full range of what is available to you, please consult the CSS specifications as well as the Online Manual for your version of AH Formatter.

Conventions used in this document

- Descriptions of CSS properties comprise much of this document. Property descriptions may include:
  - Initial value
  - Elements to which the property applies
  - Whether or not the property is inherited
  - Explanatory text
  - List of allowed values

    A property description is formatted as follows:

Incrementing Counters : 'counter-increment'

◼ Initial value: 'none'   ◼ Applies to: all elements   ◼ Inherited: no

Use the 'counter-increment' property to increase the specified counter value.

- 'none' : Does not alter any counters.
- <custom-ident> : Name of the counter to increment. The value of the specified counter increments by one.
- <custom-ident>, <integer> : Alters the counter value by the integer value. A negative integer decrements the counter value.

- Property names and property value keywords are enclosed in single quotes: for example, 'counter-increment' and 'none'.
- Pseudo-elements, rule names, and functions are also enclosed in single quotes. Their type is also given, unless it is obvious from the context: for example, "'::before' pseudo-element" and "'@page' rule".
- Element names are shown as start tags: for example, `<style>`.
- CSS fragments are shown as monospace text: for example, `float: left;`.
- When the allowed value of a property or of a function argument is a datatype, such as an integer or a percentage, the name of the datatype is shown between '<' and '>' ; for example, <integer>.
- <custom-ident> in the definition of a property's value represents an author-defined identifier. Any valid CSS identifier may be used, provided that is not a predefined CSS keyword that is valid in that context.
- The CSS level of a property, a property value, or a feature is indicated as follows:
  1. Defined by CSS 2.1: no mark
  2. Defined by CSS 3: 🔲
  3. AH Formatter extension: ◢

    CSS 3 is still under development. Some properties defined in previous CSS 3 Working Drafts are no longer included in current Working Drafts. The CSS 3 specifications may continue to change in the future.

CSS 3 properties can be used with or without an -ah- prefix. AH Formatter extension properties will not operate properly unless you include the -ah- prefix.

- Emphasized text is shown as text with a yellow background.
- Blocks of sample markup or sample CSS are shown in monospace text:

```
<p>Number of this page =
    <span style="content: counter(page)"></span>
</p>
<p>Total number of pages in this document=
    <span style="content: counter(pages)"></span>
</p>
```

- Samples of styled text are enclosed in a box:

Optional title
Number of this page = 4 Total number of pages in this document = 204

- Cross-references are shown as green text.

Feedback

Help us to improve this document. Please send any comments, corrections, or suggestions for improvement to support@antennahouse.com.

SCREEN & PAGED MEDIA

'@media' Rule

An '@media' conditional group rule contains a set of CSS style sheet rules that are specific to a target medium. Specify `@media print` for rules that are specific to paged media and `@media screen` for rules that are specific to screen display.[1]

```
@media print {          /* applies to paged media */
  body {
    margin: 0;
    font-size: 10pt;
  }
}

@media screen {         /* applies to screen display */
  body {
    margin: 10%;
    font-size: 12px;
  }
}

body {                  /* applies to all media */
  font-family: sans-serif;
}
```

Specifying a Print Style Sheet

`<style>` element

A `<style>` element contains style information for the document. In HTML 4.01, `<style>` may only appear inside `<head>`. In HTML 5, `<style>` may also be used in the body of the document.

---

1 Since AH Formatter is print formatting software, the AH Formatter GUI applies `@media print` rules and does not apply `@media screen` rules.

```
<style type="text/css" media="print">
…
</style>
```

'@import' rule

A print-only style sheet can be created in another CSS file by including it with '@import'.

```
@import url("PrintOnly.css") print; /* PrintOnly.css printing */
```

`media` attribute of `<style>` and `<link>` elements

Specifying print as the media attribute value links the print style sheet with the `<style>` or `<link>` element.

```
<link rel="stylesheet" type="text/css" media="print" href="foo.css">
```

Differences Between Screen and Paged Media

Design approach

Screen display and printing (or any sort of paged media) require different approaches to designing the layout.

The size and aspect ratio of a screen display may change depending on the display environment, so it is hard to know how to accurately specify the size and arrangement of the layout target. The style specification should consider using relative dimensions to accommodate various environments.

In printing, there is an expectation that formatted objects are arranged neatly on fixed-sized pages, therefore, the layout specification should precisely control the layout by specifying absolute dimensions for the size and position of the formatting objects, starting with the size of its characters.

Breaks

Breaks happen in both paged and unpaged documents. For example, text is broken into lines, and the text in a block that has 'column-count' greater than one may be broken into columns. However, and unsurprisingly, breaks are more common, and more of a concern, when a run of text is also broken across pages. There are properties for forcing or avoiding breaks within or between elements. Additionally, the 'widows' and 'orphans' properties control the minimum number of lines of text before or after a break in a block of text.

Floats

In unpaged media, a box can float to the left or right. In paged media, it can also float to the top or bottom of the page (and AH Formatter implements more detailed control over floats). Items that you might float include graphics, sidebars, and footnotes.

Navigation

Paged media (i.e., books) have well-developed conventions for navigating between pages.

Pages are typically numbered, and, often, the front matter is numbered in a different style and sequence to the main text.

The page number and, often, the book, chapter or even section title may appear at the periphery of the page. Dictionaries have their own conventions for indicating the first and last entries on each page. CSS defines 16 regions around the edge of the page for presenting this sort of information.

The table of contents (or tables of contents) and index facilitate non-sequential access.

A chapter (or other significant division) may start on a right-hand page (for left-to-right writing mode documents), and the chapter start may have a different appearance to other pages (and possibly different headers and footers).

Left and right pages

A document that is printed on both sides of the page and bound into a book-like form (even a document that is duplex-printed on an office printer and placed in a folder) will form two-page spreads with a left-hand and a right-hand page. Also, because a book is bound, it is easier to see the details near the outer edges of each page as you leaf through the document than it is to see the inner edges of the page near the binding. Thirdly, the sequential reading order of the pages makes it convenient to think of each two-sided leaf of the document as having a 'front' and a 'back' side.

All of these aspects can affect the page design. For example, chapter openings are typically (but not exclusively) on the right-hand of a spread, since that is the 'front' side of a leaf. Page numbers and any other navigation aids on a page are more likely to be on or near the outer edge of each page so they can be seen more easily when leafing through the document. Thinking of the document as a sequence of two-page spreads also raises questions of whether the facing pages should be symmetrical around the gutter and whether items such as graphics can span across the two pages.

The printed book

Several things should be considered for a document that is to be printed rather than only viewed on screen.

There may be constraints on the page size. A document that is meant to be printed by the end user may be sized to suit the paper size of an office printer: Letter size in the USA; A4 in most of the rest of the world; or A4 or JIS-B5 in Japan. A car handbook, on the other hand, is usually a convenient size for a car glove compartment. Trade paperbacks have a range of conventional sizes, and choosing an unconventional page size could affect the sales of a book.

If the paper is not sufficiently opaque, the text on the opposite side of the paper may show through. The effect is made worse if the text on each side of the paper is not aligned.

Introduction to CSS for Paged Media

Using CSS in paged media design for XML and HTML is not yet common but its use is expected to increase as the development of CSS 3 progresses. This tutorial aims to make CSS for Paged Media easy to understand.

Introduction to CSS for Paged Media

Using CSS in paged media design for XML and HTML is not yet common but its use is expected to increase as the development of CSS 3 progresses. This tutorial aims to make CSS for Paged Media easy to understand.

Effect of show-through with non-aligned and aligned text

Graphics, and other design elements, that extend to the edge of the page may need to be printed so they extend past the edge of the page (see 3. PAGE LAYOUT (page 21)). If they do not bleed past the edge of the page, then any inaccuracy when trimming the page to its correct size after printing and binding could result in a white strip between the graphic and the edge of the page. Conversely, the graphic should not have significant details close to the edge of page in case the trimming takes off too much rather than too little.

Even the binding method may need to be considered when designing the book. Perfect binding or a wire binding may reduce the visible or usable area of the gutter between pages. If the pages of a book are gathered into signatures and then trimmed, the pages in the middle of the signature may have more trimmed from their fore-edge than is trimmed from the pages on the outside of the signature.

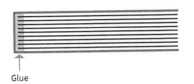

Glue

Gutter reduced by perfect binding

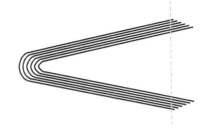

Fore-edge reduced by trimming of signature

Effect of binding method

BOX LAYOUT

In CSS, everything is a box. The tree of elements and text that makes up the document is transformed into a tree of boxes. Some elements generate multiple boxes: for example, an `<li>`. Some generate none: for example, elements such as `<col>` or any element with `display: none;`.

Box Model

The broadest classification of boxes is that there are block-level boxes, line boxes, and inline-level boxes. A block-level box, such as for a paragraph, contains either other block-level boxes or it contains line boxes. A paragraph containing only text generates a block-level box that contains line boxes. A list generates a block-level box that contains a block-level box for each list item. A paragraph that contains text plus a list generates one anonymous box around each of the line boxes for the text plus the block-level box for the list. The anonymous boxes ensure that no box contains both block-level boxes and line boxes. A line box contains one or more inline-level boxes, since every change of font or style generates a separate inline-level box.

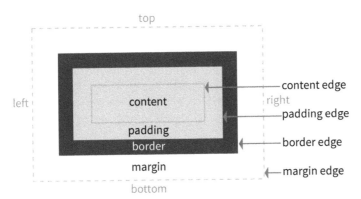

Areas and edges of a CSS box

2

To format this markup:

```
<div>
   Some text
   <p>More text</p>
</div>
```

the formatter generates an anonymous box around 'Some text' to ensure that the block box for the `<div>` does not contain both an inline box and a block box.

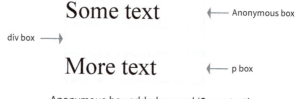

Anonymous box added around 'Some text'

Every box has a content area, and the bounds of the content area are the content edge. The padding area is around the content area, and it is bounded by the padding edge. Similarly, the border surrounds the padding, and the margin surrounds the border. Some boxes have zero-width padding, border, or margin on one or more sides, either because of the CSS definition of the areas generated for a box type or because the corresponding properties are set to zero.

Box Display and Printing

Boxes are laid out in a hierarchical structure starting with a box at the top for the root element down to a box containing the lowest character string. When the output destination is the screen, the root element box is displayed on the screen. When the output destination is paged media, an '@page' rule determines the page box, and the boxes for the elements are placed inside the page box.

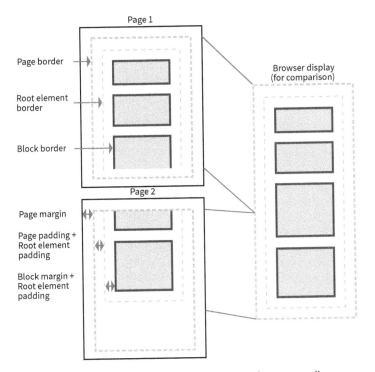

Comparison of boxes generated for page and screen media

Display Format : 'display'

Initial value: 'inline'   Applies to: all elements   Inherited: no

Use the 'display' property to control how an element is displayed.

The 'display' property changes only the display format of the element, not its role.

- 'block' : Generate a block box.
- 'inline-block' : Generate an inline-level block container.
- 'inline' : Generate one or more inline boxes.
- 'list-item' : Generate a principal box and a marker box.
- 'none' : Cause the element to not appear.
- 'table', 'inline-table', 'table-row-group', 'table-column', 'table-column-group', 'table-header-group', 'table-footer-group', 'table-row', 'table-cell', and 'table-caption' : Behave like a table element. See 9. TABLES (page 71).

Box Arrangement

Boxes other than in tables have a content area, surrounded by padding, border, and margin areas. Layout characteristics are specified according to their specific properties. When the hierarchical structure is laid out as page box, root element box, and block box, then the content, padding, and border are arranged as shown in the following figure. For information on tables, please refer to 9. TABLES (page 71).

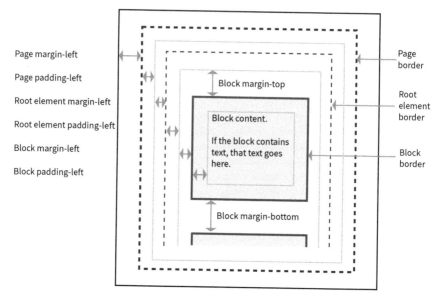

Page margin-left

Page padding-left

Root element margin-left

Root element padding-left

Block margin-left

Block padding-left

Block margin-top

Block content.

If the block contains text, that text goes here.

Block margin-bottom

Page border

Root element border

Block border

Box Arrangement

Box Dimensions

The size of the box is the sum of the specific values of width, height, padding, border, and margin of its content. The padding, border, and margin for the four sides may be specified together using the 'padding', 'border' (or 'border-width'), and 'margin' properties, respectively. The padding, border, and margin may also be separately specified for each side by using individual properties.

Content width : 'width'
■ Initial value: 'auto' ■ Applies to: all elements[1] ■ Inherited: no
Specifies content width.
- 'auto' : Depends on the values of other properties
- <length> : Specifies the width of the content area using a length unit.
- <percentage> : Specifies the width of the content area as a percentage of the width of the generated box's containing block.

---

1 The inline element width including table rows, strings, etc, is not applicable because it is set automatically. It does apply to image elements of inline elements. The same applies to 'min-width' and 'max-width' properties.

Content minimum width : 'min-width'

■ Initial value: 0   ■ Applies to: all elements   ■ Inherited: no

Specifies the minimum content width.

- <length> : Minimum used width.
- <percentage> : Minimum used width as a percentage of the width of the generated box's containing block.

Content maximum width : 'max-width'

■ Initial value: 'none'   ■ Applies to: all elements   ■ Inherited: no

Specifies the maximum content width.

- 'none' : No limit on the width of the box.
- <length> : Maximum used width.
- <percentage> : Maximum used width as a percentage of the width of the generated box's containing block.

Content height : 'height'

■ Initial value: 'auto'   ■ Applies to: all elements[2]   ■ Inherited: no

Specifies content height.

- 'auto' : Depends on the values of other properties
- <length> : Specifies the height of the content area using a length unit.
- <percentage> : Specifies the height of the content area as a percentage of the height of the generated box's containing block.

Content minimum height : 'min-height'

■ Initial value: 0   ■ Applies to: all elements   ■ Inherited: no

Specifies the minimum content height.

- <length> : Minimum used height.
- <percentage> : Minimum used height as a percentage of the height of the generated box's containing block.

Content maximum height : 'max-height'

■ Initial value: 'none'   ■ Applies to: all elements   ■ Inherited: no

Specifies the maximum content height.

- 'none' : No limit on the height of the box.
- <length> : Maximum used height.
- <percentage> : Maximum used height as a percentage of the height of the generated box's containing block.

---

2 The inline element height including table columns, character strings, etc, is not applicable because it is set automatically. It does apply to the image of inline elements.

Padding, border, and margin shorthands

The 'padding', 'border-width', and 'margin', as well as 'border-style' and 'border-color', properties are all shorthands for setting one of the style, etc., for all four borders at once. These properties can have one to four component values. The values are set on the different sides as shown in the following 'border-color' example.

- One value : Applies to top, bottom, left, and right sides.
- Two values : First value applies to top and bottom sides; second value applies to left and right sides.
- Three values : First value applies to top side, second value to left and right sides, and third value to bottom side.
- Four values : The values apply to top, right, bottom, and left sides, respectively.

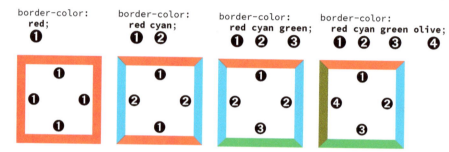

The 'border' property is a shorthand for setting the style, width, and color for all four borders. There are also properties for setting the style, width, and color of one border as well as for setting one of the style, etc., for one border only.

Padding width : 'padding'

■ Initial value: 0   ■ Applies to: all elements[3]   ■ Inherited: no

Specifies the padding width corresponding to to 'padding-top', 'padding-right', 'padding-bottom', and 'padding-left'. Allows you to simultaneously specify padding for four sides.

- <length> : Specifies the padding of the side or sides using a length unit.
- <percentage> : Specifies the padding of the side or sides as a percentage of the width of the generated box's containing block.

Border width (thickness) : 'border-width'

■ Initial value: 0   ■ Applies to: all elements   ■ Inherited: no

Specifies the border width of the top and bottom and left and right to 'border-top-width', 'border-bottom-width', 'border-left-width', 'border-right-width'. Allows you to simultaneously specify the border width for four sides.

---

3 Not applicable to table rows, columns, table headers, or footers.

Specifies color with 'border-color' and line type (style) with 'border-style' for border.

'border-top', 'border-bottom', 'border-left', and 'border-right' simultaneously specify the border width, color, and line type of the top and bottom and left and right, respectively. 'border' allows you to simultaneously specify the four sides of width, color, and line type.

Please refer to 18. BORDERS & BACKGROUND (page 143) for details on how to specify width, color, or line type of a border.

Margin thickness : 'margin'
■ Initial value: 0　■ Applies to: most elements　■ Inherited: no

Specifies the thickness of the top and bottom and left and right margins for 'margin-top', 'margin-bottom', 'margin-left', and 'margin-right'. Simultaneously allows you to specify the margin for four sides.

The margin value may be negative. The edge with a negative margin extends out from the containing box.

Changing the box model : 'box-sizing'
■ Initial value: 'content-box'　■ Applies to: all elements that accept 'width' or 'height'　■ Inherited: no

Specifies whether any padding and border are drawn inside or outside the specified width and height. Does not apply when the 'width' or 'height' value is 'auto'.

- 'content-box' : The specified width and height apply to the content box of the element.
- 'border-box' : The specified width and height apply to the border box of the element.

```
<div style="width: 60%; box-sizing: content-box; …">
  <p style="background-color: silver; text-align: center">…</p></div>
<p style="border-top: thick solid #003919; width: 60%; …"/>
<div style="width: 60%; box-sizing: border-box; …">
  <p style="background-color: silver; text-align: center">…</p></div>
<div style="width: auto; box-sizing: content-box; …">
  <p style="background-color: silver; text-align: center">…</p></div>
<div style="width: auto; box-sizing: border-box; …">
  <p style="background-color: silver; text-align: center">…</p></div>
```

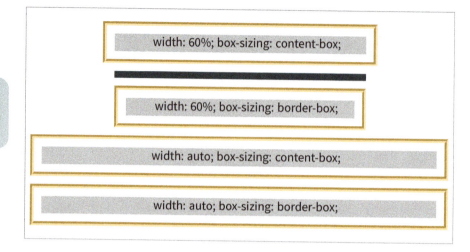

Positioning

A CSS box may be laid out according to three positioning schemes:

1. Normal flow. In CSS 2.1, normal flow includes block formatting of block-level boxes, inline formatting of inline-level boxes, and relative positioning of block-level and inline-level boxes.

2. Floats. In the float model, a box is first laid out according to the normal flow, then taken out of the flow and shifted to a different position on the same page or a following page. Depending on the size and position of the floated content, other content may flow along the side of a float. See 14. IMAGE POSITIONING (page 109).

3. Absolute positioning. In the absolute positioning model, a box is removed from the normal flow entirely (it has no impact on later siblings) and assigned a position with respect to a containing block.

An element is called 'out of flow' if it is floated, absolutely positioned, or is the root element. An element is called 'in-flow' if it is not out-of-flow.

Positioning scheme : 'position'

■Initial value: 'static'   ■Applies to: all elements   ■Inherited: no

Specifies how a CSS box that is not floated is positioned.

- 'static' : Box is a normal box. The 'top', 'bottom', 'left', and 'right' properties do not apply.
- 'relative' : Box's position is calculated according to the normal flow. The box is then offset relative to its normal position. The position of the following box is calculated as though the current box was not offset.
- 'absolute' : Box's position and possibly size are specified with the 'top', 'bottom', 'left', and 'right' properties. These properties specify offsets with respect to the

box's containing block. Absolutely positioned boxes are taken out of the normal flow. This means they have no impact on the layout of later siblings.
- 'fixed' : Box's position is calculated according to the 'absolute' model, but in addition, the box is fixed with respect to the page box.

Box offsets : 'top'/ 'bottom'/ 'left'/ 'right'

▓ Initial value: 'static'   ▓ Applies to: all elements   ▓ Inherited: no
Specifies the offsets of a relatively or absolutely positioned box.
- 'auto' : .
- <length> : The offset is a fixed distance from the reference edge. Negative values are allowed.
- <percentage> : The offset is a percentage of the containing block's width (for 'left' or 'right') or height (for 'top' and 'bottom'). Negative values are allowed.

Specifying the stack level : 'z-index'

▓ Initial value: 'auto'   ▓ Applies to: positioned elements   ▓ Inherited: no
Each box has a position in three dimensions. In addition to their horizontal and vertical positions, boxes lie along a 'z-axis' and are formatted one on top of the other.
- 'auto' : The stack level of the generated box in the current stacking context is 0. The box does not establish a new stacking context unless it is the root element.
- <integer> : Stack level of the generated box in the current context.

2

PAGE LAYOUT

In paged media, the document is formatted as one or more page boxes. The content area of a page box is called the page area. The margin area of a page box is used for headers and footers.

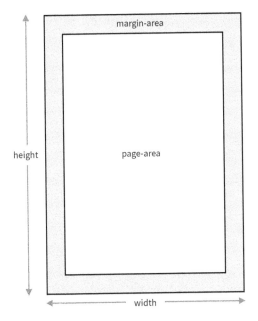

Page and Margin Area

Western Page Design

Western page design traditionally places the center of the page area above the center of the page. This is because the optical center of the page is considered to be above the geometric center. Also, the gutter margin is traditionally narrower than the fore-edge margin. This is to make it easier for the eye to move from one page to the other. The wider fore-edge allows room for the thumbs to hold the page. The two gutter margins, taken together, balance the wider fore-edge margin. Unlike Japanese page design, this places the center of the page area above and inwards from the geometric center of the page. Additionally, in a classically proportioned page, the height of the page area matches the width of the page.

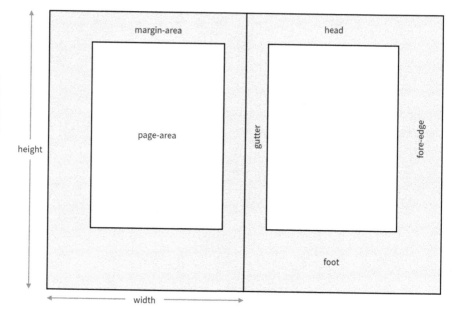

Traditional Western page design

In practice, page designs vary quite a lot. The printed 'page' now includes invoices, bank statements, package inserts for medications, marketing brochures, children's books, parts catalogs, and much more besides. The economics of printing or the need to print on A4 or Letter size paper on an office printer can influence the page design. Asymmetric page design, where the page area has the same position on facing pages, was once a radical idea but now is not uncommon. Furthermore, novels, in particular, are often sold in multiple editions with different page sizes that each reuse the same page areas with reduced margins.

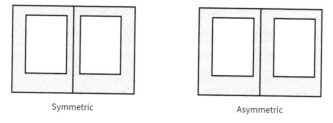

Symmetric and asymmetric spreads

Japanese Page Design

Japanese can be formatted either with horizontal lines of text and pages progressing from left to right or with vertical lines of text and pages progressing from right to left. Some formatted documents mix the two. Different types of publication are predominately one writing mode or the other: for example, government documentation and educational materials both predominately use horizontal text, whereas novels predominately use vertical text.

For both writing modes, the page area is typically centered on the page media and has proportions similar to the proportions of the media. *Requirements for Japanese Text Layout* recommends that the best line length is around 52 characters per line for vertical text and around 40 characters per line for horizontal text. However, in reality, the best line length depends on multiple factors, including the character size and the page size.

In Japanese text composition, it is common to set the width of the page area in fullwidth characters. Using em for the 'width' property in the '@page' rule sets the width in characters. Setting the left and right margin values to 'auto' aligns the page area in the center of the page.

```
@page {
  size: A4;
  /* set width of page area to multiple of character size */
  width: 43em;
  margin-top: 30mm;
  margin-bottom: 30mm;
  /* Position page area in the horizontal center of the page */
  margin-left: auto;
  margin-right: auto;
}
```

@page Rule

An '@page' rule sets basic settings such as page size, margin, page header, and page footer.

```
@page {
  size:    A4;
  margin: 25mm;
  @top-center {
    content: "Sample";
  }
  @bottom-center {
    content: counter(page);
  }
}
```

Page Size : 'size' 🔲

🔲 Initial value: 'auto'   🔲 Applies to: '@page'   🔲 Inherited: no

Specifies the width and height of the page box.

- 'auto' : Size and orientation chosen by the UA.
- <length>{1,2} : One length value sets both the height and width of the page box. Two length values set the page box width and height, respectively.
- <paper-size> : Defined page name, such as 'A4' or 'Letter'. Size names are case-insensitive.

<paper-size>	Width×Height	Source
'A3'	297×420mm	ISO 216
'A4'	210×297mm	ISO 216
'A5'	148×210mm	ISO 216
'A6'	105×148mm	ISO 216
'B4'	250×353mm	ISO 216
'ISO-B4'	250×353mm	ISO 216
'JIS-B4'	257×364mm	JIS P 0138
'B5'	176×250mm	ISO 216
'ISO-B5'	176×250mm	ISO 216
'JIS-B5'	182×257mm	JIS P 0138
'B6'	125×176mm	ISO 216
'ISO-B6'	125×176mm	ISO 216
'JIS-B6'	128×182mm	JIS P 0138
'Letter'	8.5×11in	North American Paper Sizes
'Government-Letter'	8×10.5in	North American Paper Sizes
'Legal'	8.5×14in	North American Paper Sizes
'Ledger'	17×11in	North American Paper Sizes
'Tabloid'	11×17in	North American Paper Sizes
'Statement'	5.5×8.5in	

<paper-size>	Width×Height	Source
'Executive'	7.25×10.5in	
'Folio'	210×330mm	
'C'	17×22in	ANSI Paper Sizes
'D'	22×34in	ANSI Paper Sizes
'E'	34×44in	ANSI Paper Sizes
'ISO-DL'	110×220mm	ISO 269
'ISO-C3'	324×458mm	ISO 269
'ISO-C4'	229×324mm	ISO 269
'ISO-C5'	162×229mm	ISO 269
'ISO-C6'	114×162mm	ISO 269
'Hagaki'	100×148mm	Japan Post Co., Ltd.

- 'portrait' : Print the page's content in portrait orientation.
- 'landscape' : Print the pages content in landscape orientation.

```
@page {
  size: 6in 9in;
}
```

```
@page {
  size: 210mm 297mm; ; /* ISO/JIS A4 */
}
```

Defined page names such as 'A5', 'A4', 'A3', 'B5', 'B4', 'JIS-B5', 'JIS-B4', 'letter', 'legal', and 'ledger' can be used for 'size' property.

```
@page {
  size: A4; /* ISO/JIS A4 (210mm×297mm) */
}
```

```
@page {
  size: letter; /* North American 'Letter' paper size */
}
```

```
@page {
  size: JIS-B5; /* JIS B5 (182mm×257mm) */
}
```

Landscape orientation can be specified by adding the 'landscape' keyword to the page size specification.

```
@page {
  size: A4 landscape;    /* A4 landscape (297mm×210mm) */
}
```

Page Margin : 'margin'

◼ Initial value: See individual properties ◼ Applies to: all elements
◼ Inherited: no

The 'margin' property is a shorthand for 'margin-top', 'margin-bottom', 'margin-left', and 'margin-right'.

- When there is one value : The margin value applies to (up, down, left, right).
- When there are two values : The margin values apply to (top, bottom) and (left, right).
- When there are three values : The margin values apply to top, left/right, and bottom.
- When there are four values : The margin values apply to top, right, bottom, left.

Specify page margins with the 'margin' property on a '@page' rule.

```
@page {
  margin: 10%;    /* Top, bottom, left, right margins each take up
                     10% of the page width */
}
```

```
@page {
  /* Top/bottom margins are set to 2cm and left/right are set to
     3cm */
  margin-top: 2cm;
  margin-bottom: 2cm;
  margin-left: 3cm;
  margin-right: 3cm;
}
```

If not specified, the initial value of margin-* is zero[1]. margin-* specified on the (X)HTML body element is taken inside the page area. If margin-* is specified for both '@page' and html (including body element) elements in (X)HTML, the margins are added together.

---

[1] In AH Formatter, the initial value can be set to any value. Since the default page margin value is set to 2 cm, the initial value will not be zero.

Named Page : 'page' ⬛

⬛ Initial value: 'auto'   ⬛ Applies to: boxes that create class 1 break points
⬛ Inherited: no

Several types of named '@page' rules can be created, and the 'page' property enables switching between them within one document.

- 'auto' : The used value is the value specified on the nearest ancestor with a non-auto value.
- <identifier> : The named page on which the element must be displayed.
- <identifier>+ auto+ 🔲 : As content is laid out and new pages are generated, the list is traversed linearly starting at the first list item. One page is created per item in the list. If more pages are required than there are items in the list, the last item is repeated as many times as necessary.[2]

```
@page Landscape {    /* "Landscape" named page */
  size: A4 landscape;
}
@page Portrait {     /* "Portrait" named page */
  size: A4;
}
table.WideTable {
  page: Landscape;   /* Place a large table on a "Landscape" page */
}
html {
  page: Portrait;    /* Use a "Portrait" page as the default */
}
```

```
<p>Portrait page</p>

<table class="WideTable" border="1" style="width:100%">
<tr>
<td>1</td>
...
<td>18</td>
</tr>
</table>
```

3

---

2 This was defined in a previous GCPM Working Draft but has since been removed.

Portrait page

1 2 3 4 5 6 7 8 9 10 11 12 13 14 15 16 17 18

'page' property selects a named page

Constraining The Number of Pages : '-ah-force-page-count'

■ Initial value: 'auto'   ■ Applies to: CSS '@page' without any selectors[3]
■ Inherited: no

Imposes a constraint on the total number of pages for the document. If the constraint is not satisfied, an additional page (or additional pages) will be added at the end of the document. Reasons for constraining the number of page include: an office document printed on both sides of the paper may need an even number of pages; a document printed as a booklet may need a multiple of four pages; or a document printed by a commercial printer may be printed with 8, 16, 32, or 64 pages on one sheet of paper that is then folded and trimmed to become part of a book.

- 'auto' : Do not force any page count.
- 'even' : Force an even number of pages.
- 'odd' : Force an odd number of pages.
- 'doubly-even' : Force a doubly-even (multiple of four) number of pages.
- 'end-on-even' : Force the last page to be an even page.
- 'end-on-odd' : Force the last page to be an odd page.
- 'end-on-doubly-even' : Force the last page to be a doubly-even page.
- 'even-document' : Force the last page to be an even page.
- 'odd-document' : Force the last page to be an odd page.
- 'doubly-even-document' : Force the last page to be a doubly-even page.
- [end-on | document] <number> [<number>] : Force the number of pages to be a multiple of the first number plus the second number, if present.[4]
- 'no-force' : Do not force either an even number or an odd number of pages.

For example, if the document would generate 5 pages:

- `-ah-force-page-count: even;`
  Equivalent to `-ah-force-page-count: 2;`.

---

3 This restriction may be removed in a future AH Formatter version.
4 This feature is not available in AH Formatter Lite.

- `-ah-force-page-count: odd;`
    Equivalent to `-ah-force-page-count: 2 1;`.
- `-ah-force-page-count: doubly-even;`
    Equivalent to `-ah-force-page-count: 4;`.
- `-ah-force-page-count: end-on-doubly-even;`
    Equivalent to `-ah-force-page-count: end-on 4;`.
- `-ah-force-page-count: end-on 2;`
    Total number of pages is 6 with 1 blank page.
- `-ah-force-page-count: end-on 4;`
    Total number of pages is 8 with 3 blank page.
- `-ah-force-page-count: end-on 4 1;`
    Total number of pages is 5 with 0 blank pages.
- `-ah-force-page-count: end-on 4 3;`
    Total number of pages is 7 with 2 blank pages.
- `-ah-force-page-count: end-on 6 5;`
    Total number of pages is 5 with 0 blank pages.
- `-ah-force-page-count: end-on 6 4;`
    Total number of pages is 10 with 5 blank pages.

Crop and Registration Marks[5]

An '@page' rule defines a page box, but the page box may be printed on a page sheet that is larger than the page box. A common reason for this is so images and other content can extend up to the edge of the page box. A physical device such as a printer typically has a non-printable area around the edge of the page sheet where it is not capable of printing reliably, if at all. Printing the page box on a larger page sheet then trimming the page sheet to the size of the page box avoids problems with the non-printable area. Extending images, etc., into the bleed area outside the page box avoids problems if the trimming to size is inaccurate.

Crop and registration marks are printed outside the page box and are used as guides when trimming the page sheet to size and for checking that content printed on both sides of a duplex sheet is aligned correctly. Other information that may be printed outside the page box includes color bars for checking color fidelity as well as information identifying the page, its containing document, its version number, etc.

---

5 The crop mark feature is not available in AH Formatter Lite.

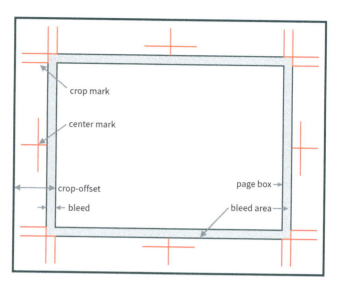

Crop mark terms

Printer marks display : 'marks'

Initial value: 'none'   Applies to: CSS '@page'   Inherited: no

Specifies whether to print crop marks when printing.

- 'crop' : Outputs crop marks.
- 'crop-trim' : Outputs only corner marks
- 'cross' : Outputs cross marks and registration marks.
- 'cross-circle' : Outputs cross-shaped marks with a concentric circle
- 'cross-registration' : Outputs registration marks
- <uri-specification> : Location of an SVG, or similar, image representing custom printer marks, color bars, etc. Multiple images can be specified.

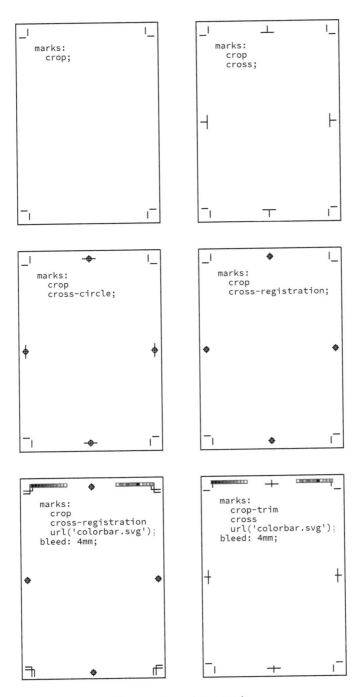

```
marks:
  crop;
```

```
marks:
  crop
  cross;
```

```
marks:
  crop
  cross-circle;
```

```
marks:
  crop
  cross-registration;
```

```
marks:
  crop
  cross-registration
  url('colorbar.svg');
bleed: 4mm;
```

```
marks:
  crop-trim
  cross
  url('colorbar.svg');
bleed: 4mm;
```

Cross marks and crop marks

You can output crop marks at the four corners and/or cross marks at the centers of the four sides of the page box. Crop marks indicate the alignment for cutting to the finished size, and cross marks can help with registration for multi-color printing as well as for registration between the front and back of a duplex sheet. You can also or alternatively output custom printer marks by specifying the location of one or more external images.

The printer marks feature is not available in AH Formatter Lite.

```
@page {
    size: B5; /* ISO B5 (176mm 250mm) */
    margin: 28mm 21.325mm;
    marks: crop cross;           /* printer marks to display */
    -ah-crop-offset: 14mm;       /* distance from the page box edge to
                                    the page sheet edge */
    -ah-printer-marks-line-color: auto; /* printer marks line color*/
    -ah-printer-marks-line-length: 8mm; /* printer marks line length*/
    -ah-printer-marks-line-width: 0.2mm;/* printer marks line width*/
    bleed: 3mm;                  /* page bleed distance */
}
```

Printer marks visibility : '-ah-crop-area-visibility'
■ Initial value: 'hidden' ■ Applies to: CSS '@page' ■ Inherited: no
Specifies whether to display the area that extends beyond the finished page size.
- 'hidden' : Crop area is hidden.
- 'visible' : Crop area is visible.

Printer marks line color : '-ah-printer-marks-line-color'
■ Initial value: 'auto' ■ Applies to: CSS '@page' ■ Inherited: no
Specifies the line color of printer marks. See 17. COLOR (page 135) for details. When the value is 'auto', the registration color is used.

Printer marks line length : '-ah-printer-marks-line-length'
■ Initial value: 'auto' ■ Applies to: CSS '@page' ■ Inherited: no
Specifies the line length of printer marks. When the value is 'auto', the length is dependent on the system setting. The printer mark default length is 10mm, but this can be adjusted in the AH Formatter Option Setting File.

Printer marks line width : '-ah-printer-marks-line-width'
■ Initial value: 'auto' ■ Applies to: CSS '@page' ■ Inherited: no
Specifies the line width of printer marks. When the value is 'auto', the length is dependent on the system setting. The printer mark default width is 0.2pt, but this can be adjusted in the AH Formatter Option Setting File.

Distance from the end to the trim size of the output medium : '-ah-crop-offset' ▨◢

▨ Initial value: 0 ▨ Applies to: CSS '@page' ▨ Inherited: no

Specifies the distance from the physical end to the trim size of the output medium.

Page Bleed Area

A graphic, or similar, may *bleed off* (or be *bled-out* from) the cut edge of the page. Extending an image to the edge of the page is often a useful effect. If the image extends just to the edge of the trimmed page, inaccurate trimming could leave a white area along the outer edge of the image. Extending the image past the edge of the page then trimming to size avoids problems from inaccuracy when trimming.

Page bleed

Inaccurate trimming may trim too much or too little. When a graphic bleeds off the edge of the page, the most significant parts of the graphic should not be too close to the page edge in case they are trimmed.

Bleeds should anticipate that too much could be trimmed as well as too little

Differences in trimming of successive pages of a commercially printed book

Bleed region width : 'bleed'

■ Initial value: 0 ■ Applies to: '@page' ■ Inherited: no

Specifies the width of the bleed region for trimming. The value is a <length>. The bleed region extends outwards from the page box. By specifying a negative value for the margin of a page-margin box (see Page-Margin Boxes (page 35)), the margin box can be extended into the bleed region.

If the value of 'bleed' is greater than the value of '-ah-crop-offset', then '-ah-crop-offset' is adjusted to match the 'bleed' value.

Per-side Bleed Properties : 'bleed-top'/ 'bleed-right'/ 'bleed-bottom'/ 'bleed-left'

■ Initial value: 0 ■ Applies to: '@page' ■ Inherited: no

Each property specifies the width of the top, right, bottom, or left bleed region of the page. The value is a <length>. When 'bleed' is also specified, these individual '-ah-bleed-*' properties have priority.

HEADERS & FOOTERS

Headers and footers are formatted in the 16 page-margin boxes at the page edge.

Page-Margin Boxes

Page-margin boxes are named according to their position around the page, as follows: '@top-left-corner', '@top-left', '@top-center', '@top-right', '@top-right-corner', '@left-top', '@left-middle', '@left-bottom', '@right-top', '@right-middle', '@right-bottom', '@bottom-left-corner', '@bottom-left', '@bottom-center', '@bottom-right', and '@bottom-right-corner'.

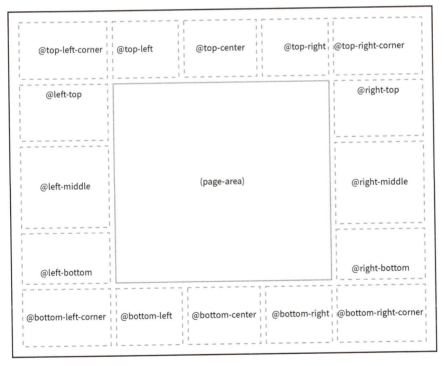

Location of each page-margin box

The page header and page footer are assigned to page-margin box areas around the page.

```
@page {
  /* page header */
  @top-right {
    content: "Sample";
  }
  /* page footer */
  @bottom-center {
    content: counter(page);
  }
}
```

Each page-margin box has a default alignment.

Default alignment for page-margin boxes

Page-margin box	'text-align'	'vertical-align'
@top-left-corner	right	middle
@top-left	left	middle
@top-center	center	middle
@top-right	right	middle
@top-right-corner	left	middle
@left-top	center	top
@left-middle	center	middle
@left-bottom	center	bottom
@right-top	center	top
@right-middle	center	middle
@right-bottom	center	bottom
@bottom-left-corner	right	middle
@bottom-left	left	middle
@bottom-center	center	middle
@bottom-right	right	middle
@bottom-right-corner	left	middle

4

Page-margin box dimensions

A page-margin box that has content is 'generated' and is considered in width or height calculations. Otherwise, no box is generated for it, similarly to an element with `display: none;`.

How to determine the dimensions of a page-margin box (for which the 'width' and 'height' properties are both 'auto') can be divided into three categories:

- @top-left, @top-right, @bottom-left, @bottom-right : The dimensions of the containing block are determined by the margins that intersect at that corner.

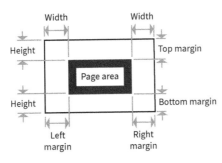

Dimensions of corner page-margin boxes

- @top-left, @top-center, @top-right, @bottom-left, @bottom-center, @bottom-right
    - Width is determined by considering the relative minimum and maximum formatted widths of each of the page-margin boxes on that side and dividing the available width accordingly. If the center page-margin box is generated, it will always be centered in the available width, and the left and right page-margin boxes will have equal width. Otherwise, all of the available width is divided between the left and right page-margin boxes.

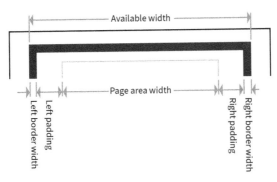

Available width for horizontal left, center, and right page-margin boxes

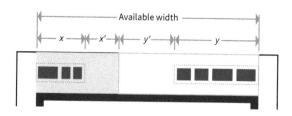

Page-margin box width depends on content

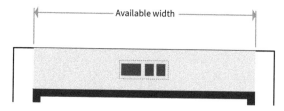

Single page-margin box uses full available width

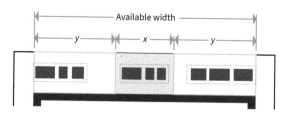

Center page-margin box is always centered

- ▫ Height is determined by the used page margin.
- ▪ @left-top, @left-middle, @left-bottom, @right-top, @right-middle, @right-bottom
  - ▫ Width is determined by the used page margin.
  - ▫ Height is determined by considering the relative minimum and maximum formatted heights of each of the page-margin boxes on that side and dividing the available height accordingly. If the middle page-margin box is generated, it will always be centered in the available height, and the top and bottom page-margin boxes will have equal height. Otherwise, all of the available height is divided between the left and right page-margin boxes.

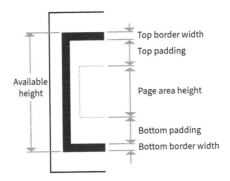

Available height for vertical top, middle, and bottom page-margin boxes

The 'width', 'min-width', 'max-width', 'height', 'min-height', and 'max-height' properties apply to page-margin boxes and can affect or override the default calculations:

- Specifying 'width' or 'height' directly determines the width or height, respectively, of the page-margin box. The width, or height, of related page-margin boxes with `width: auto;` or `height: auto;` are resolved such that the page-margin boxes fill the available width.

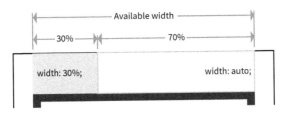

Fixed-width page-margin box

- Specifying 'max-width' (or 'max-height') may cause the initial division of space to be revised: if any of the page-margin boxes exceed their specified 'max-width' (or 'max-height') value, then the calculation is repeated using the specified value

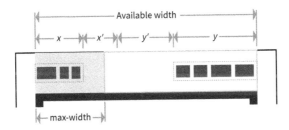

'max-width' and 'min-width' may alter page-margin box widths

- Specifying 'min-width' (or 'min-height') may cause the current result to be revised: if any of the page-margin boxes are less than their specified 'min-width' (or 'min-height') value, then the calculation is repeated using the specified value.

Page-margin box properties

See PAGE BOX AND PAGE-MARGIN BOX CSS PROPERTIES (page 174) for the CSS properties that apply to a page-margin box. AH Formatter provides some additional properties.

Running Headers and Page Numbers

Running header setting : 'string-set' property and 'string()' function 🔲

Character strings from the headings in the main body can be displayed in the page header.

```
@page {
  @top-left {
    /* Use the value of the 'Chapter' named string. */
    content: string(Chapter);
  }
}

/* Set the value of the 'Chapter' named string. */
h1 { string-set: Chapter content(); }
```

Variable strings : 'string-set' 🔲

■ Initial value: 'none'   ■ Applies to: all elements, but not pseudo-elements
■ Inherited: no

Use the 'string-set' property to make a named variable for a string. The 'string-set' value is pairs of a variable name and followed by the content list stored in the named string. Strings defined with 'string-set' can be referenced in running headers.
- 'none' : No named strings are created.
- <custom-ident> <content-list> : The value of <content-list> becomes the text content of the string named by <custom-ident>. Multiple <custom-ident> and <content-list> pairs may be specified separated by commas.

The content list may be one or more of the following, in any order:
- <string> : A string.
- <counter()> : A 'counter()' function. See 16. COUNTERS (page 125) for details.
- <counters()> : A 'counters()' function.
- <content()> : A 'content()' function. Allowed values are:
  - content() : string value of the element.
  - content(before) : string value of the '::before' pseudo-element.
  - content(after) : string value of the '::after' pseudo-element.

- content(first-letter) : first letter of the element.
- attr(<attr-name>) : string value of the attribute <attr-name>.
- -ah-attr-from(<from-name>, <attr-name> <type-or-unit>? [, <fallback>]?) : string value of the attribute <attr-name> on the ancestor <from-name> element. ◪

```
h1 {
  /* Use the contents of h1:before and h1 as the content
     of the 'Chapter' named string.  Void the 'Section'
     named string. */
  string-set: Chapter content(before) content(), Section "";
}
```

'string()' 🗒

Used to copy the value of a named string into the document.

Strings defined with a 'string-set' value are referenced as, for example, content: string(Chapter); in running headers.

The required first value is the name of the string.

```
/* Title in right-hand page header. */
@top-right {
  content: string(Chapter);
}
```

If multiple elements on one page each set the value of the same named string, then the named string may have several values on that page. The optional second argument of 'string()' specifies which of the possible values to use:

- 'start' : use the named string's entry value (the assignment in effect at the end of the previous page) for that page.
- 'first' : if there are any assignments on the page, use the value of the first assignment, otherwise use the entry value.
- 'last' : use the named string's exit value (the assignment in effect at the end of the current page) for the page.
- 'first-except' : similar to 'first', except that the empty string is used on the page where the value is assigned. This can be used, for example, to not repeat the chapter title in the header of the first page of a chapter.

```
@page Index:right {
  @top-left {
    /* First index term on the page. */
    content: string(IndexTerm, first);
  }

  @top-right {
    /* Last index term on the page. */
```

```
        content: string(IndexTerm, last);
    }
}
```

Move elements to header/footer : 'running()' position value 📑

Use `position: running(name);` to make an element available for display in a page-margin box. The 'name' the name by which the element is referred to in 'element()' functions.

An element with `position: running(name);` is not shown in its natural place: it is treated as if `display: none;` had been set. The element inherits from its original position in the document, but does not display there.

```
/* Remove from main text and make available for header/footer. */
p.Title {
    /* Use as the 'Title' running element. */
    position: running(Title);
    /* Override the inherited '1em' indent for <p>.
        Otherwise, the content in the header would have the indent. */
    text-indent: 0;
}
```

Insert a running element: 'element()' 📑

Used to copy a running element into a page-margin box.

Elements taken out of their natural place using `position: running(name);` are referenced as `content: element(name);` in page-margin boxes. The content returned by 'element()' is the element, its pseudo-elements and its descendants. Unlike 'string()', 'element()' cannot be combined with any other values.

A running element inherits through its normal place in the document.

The required first value is the name of the running element.

```
/* Title in left-hand page header. */
@top-left {
    content: element(Title);
}
```

If multiple elements on one page each set the value of a running element using the same name, then the running element may have several values on that page. The optional second argument of 'element()' specifies which of the possible values to use:

- 'start' : use the running element's entry value (the assignment in effect at the end of the previous page) for that page.
- 'first' : if there are any assignments on the page, use the value of the first assignment, otherwise use the entry value.

- 'last' : use the running element's exit value (the assignment in effect at the end of the current page) for the page.
- 'first-except' : similar to 'first', except that the empty string is used on the page where the value is assigned.

Page number : counter(page) 🗐

'counter(page)' is used for generating page numbers. 'counter()' was defined by CSS 2.1, but in CSS 3, a preassigned counter for page numbers is introduced in the page context. The counter is incremented by 1 on every page of the document, unless the 'counter-increment' property in the page context explicitly specifies a different increment for the 'page' counter.

```
@page {
  @top-right {
    content: "Page " counter(page);
  }
}
```

AH Formatter allows 'physical' and 'reverse' keywords after 'page'. The generated page number is then either the physical page number or the number of pages to the end of the page sequence, respectively.

Total pages : counter(pages) 🗐

A counter named 'pages' is automatically available. Its value is always the total number of pages in the document. The value of 'pages' cannot be manipulated: 'counter-reset' and 'counter-increment' statements that set it are valid, but they have no effect.

The total page count can be output together with the current page number, for example "Page 57 of 204".

```
@page {
  @top-right {
    content: "Page " counter(page physical) " of " counter(pages);
  }
}
```

Headers and Footers Based on Page Position: ':left', ':right', ':first', and ':blank'

You can set the page margins as well as the content and style of page-margin boxes for a page based on its position or, using the ':blank' pseudo-class, based on whether or not it has any content. You can, for example, set different headers for left and right pages. These may be different again for the first page. You can also hide the titles and page number from the left-hand side of the left pages and the right-hand side of the right pages when it is the first page.

When used together with named pages, the style of the left and right pages and of the first page of each named page can be specified. The pseudo-classes may also be combined. This makes it possible, for example, to make a separate page rule for a blank left-hand page.

```css
/* left-hand page */
@page Chapter:left {
  @top-left {
    /* book title in the running head of the left page */
    content: string(Title);
  }
  @bottom-left {  /* page number */
    content: counter(page);
  }
}

/* right-hand page */
@page Chapter:right {
  @top-right {
    /* section title in the running head of the right page */
    content: string(Section);
  }
  @bottom-right { /* page number */
    content: counter(page);
  }
}

/* First page of a Chapter */
@page Chapter:first {
  /* hide page header */
  @top-right { content: none }
  @top-left  { content: none }
}

/* Blank page between Preface and ToC */
@page Preface:blank {
  @bottom-left { content: none; }
  @bottom-right { content: none; }
}
```

Additional Position Pseudo-classes: ':last' and ':only'

AH Formatter also implements ':last' and ':only' 'pseudo-classes for making page selectors that match on the last and only pages, respectively, of the document.

First Page

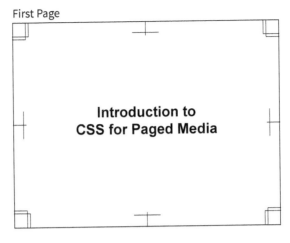

**Introduction to
CSS for Paged Media**

Right Page

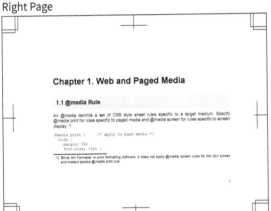

Chapter 1. Web and Paged Media

1.1 @media Rule

An @media delimits a set of CSS style sheet rules specific to a target medium. Specify @media print for rules specific to paged media and @media screen for rules specific to screen display. [1]

```
@media print {    /* apply to page media */
  body {
    margin: 5%;
    font-size: 10pt }
```

[1] Since AH Formatter is print formatting software, it does not apply @media screen rules for the GUI screen and instead applies @media print rule.

Left Page

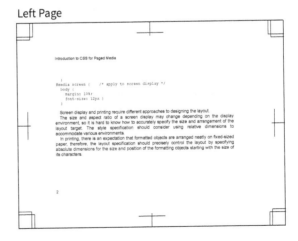

Introduction to CSS for Paged Media

```
@media screen {    /* apply to screen display */
  body {
    margin: 10%;
    font-size: 12px }
```

Screen display and printing require different approaches to designing the layout.
The size and aspect ratio of a screen display may change depending on the display environment, so it is hard to know how to accurately specify the size and arrangement of the layout target. The style specification should consider using relative dimensions to accommodate various environments.
In printing, there is an expectation that formatted objects are arranged neatly on fixed-sized paper, therefore, the layout specification should precisely control the layout by specifying absolute dimensions for the size and position of the formatting objects starting with the size of its characters.

2

4

MULTIPLE COLUMNS

CSS 3 adds the ability to format a block element as multiple columns. The 'column-count', 'column-width', and 'columns' properties, in combination, determine the number of columns that will be formatted within the available width. When there are multiple columns, specifying `column-span: all;` on a block element allows it to span across all columns.

AH Formatter implements the CSS 3 properties for controlling the gap between columns plus the optional rule that can be drawn in the column gap. It also implements addition extension properties for finer control over the appearance of the column rule.

Column count : 'column-count' ▣

■ Initial value: 'auto'   ■ Applies to: block elements   ■ Inherited: no

Specifies the number of columns of a block element.

- 'auto' : Number of columns is determined by other properties, including by specifying 'column-width' with a length value.
- <integer> : Optimal number of columns. If 'column-count' and 'column-width' both have non-auto values, then this is the maximum number of columns.

This example sets `column-count: 2;` for the block. Also specifies 'column-gap' and 'column-rule'.

```
div.MultiCol {
    column-count: 2;
    column-gap: 5mm;
    column-rule: dotted green 1mm;
}
```

An alternative method for specifying multiple columns is to set 'column-width' instead of 'column-count'. The number of columns will be set automatically based on the column width and the overall width of the page.

'column-rule' is a shorthand for properties that can be set individually as follows:

```
column-rule-style: dotted;
column-rule-color: green;
column-rule-width: 1mm;
```

Column width : 'column-width' 📑

■Initial value: 'auto'   ■Applies to: block elements   ■Inherited: no
Specifies the width of columns in multi-column elements.
- • 'auto' : Column width is determined by other properties, including by specifying 'column-count' with an integer value.
- • <length> : optimal column width.

This example sets `column-width: 12em;` for the block. Also specifies 'column-gap' and 'column-rule'.

```
div.MultiColW {
    column-width: 12em;
    column-gap: 1em;
```

```
    column-rule: solid 1pt;
}
```

An alternative method for specifying multiple columns is to set 'column-count' instead of 'column-width'.

Column number or width : 'columns' 📑

■Initial value: see individual properties   ■Applies to: block elements
■Inherited: no
This is a shorthand property for setting 'column-width' and 'column-count'. Omitted values are set to their initial values.

Column span : 'column-span' 📑

■Initial value: 'none'   ■Applies to: block elements, except floating and absolutely positioned elements   ■Inherited: no
Specifies the number of columns that an element spans.
- • 'none' : The element does not span multiple columns.
- • 'all' : The element spans across all columns.

Lorem ipsum dolor sit amet, consectetur adipiscing elit. Aliquam bibendum tincidunt pharetra. Lorem ipsum dolor

sit amet, consectetur adipiscing elit. Aliquam bibendum tincidunt pharetra.

Lorem ipsum dolor sit amet

Lorem ipsum dolor sit amet, consectetur adipiscing elit. Aliquam bibendum tincidunt pharetra. Lorem

ipsum dolor sit amet, consectetur adipiscing elit. Aliquam bibendum tincidunt pharetra.

Column gap : 'column-gap' 📑

■Initial value: 'normal'   ■Applies to: multi-column elements   ■Inherited: no
Specifies the width of the column gap.

- 'normal' : equivalent to 1em.
- <length> : length of gap between columns.

Column rule style : 'column-rule-style' ▤

▦ Initial value: 'none'　▦ Applies to: multi-column elements　▦ Inherited: no

Specifies the column rule style. The same values can be used as for specifying the style of a single border of a box. See Border Style : 'border-style' (page 144) for details.

Column rule width : 'column-rule-width' ▤

▦ Initial value: 'medium'　▦ Applies to: multi-column elements　▦ Inherited: no

Specifies column rule width. The same values can be used as for specifying the width of a single border of a box. See Border Thickness : 'border-width' (page 143) for details.

Column rule color : 'column-rule-color' ▤

▦ Initial value: current color property　▦ Applies to: multi-column elements
▦ Inherited: no

Specifies column rule color. See 17. COLOR (page 135) for details.

Column rule : 'column-rule' ▤

▦ Initial value: see individual properties　▦ Applies to: multi-column elements　▦ Inherited: no

Specifies column rule width, line type, and color.

Column rule length : '-ah-column-rule-length' ▨

▦ Initial value: 100%　▦ Applies to: multi-column elements　▦ Inherited: no

Specifies the length of the column rule.

```
column-rule-length: 60%; cen-        div.MultiCol {
ters a rule that is 60% of the height of    column-rule-length: 60%;
the column vertically within the col-    }
umn.
```

Column rule alignment : '-ah-column-rule-align' ▨

▦ Initial value: 'center'　▦ Applies to: multi-column elements　▦ Inherited: no

Specifies the vertical alignment of the column rule within the column.
- 'before' : Align top of column rule with top of column.
- 'center' : Center column rule within column height.
- 'after' : Align bottom of column rule with bottom of column.

```
-ah-column-rule-length:  60%;          div.MultiCol {
plus    -ah-column-rule-align:            -ah-column-rule-length: 60%;
after; aligns a rule that is 60% of the       -ah-column-rule-align: after;
height of the column with the bottom        }
of the column.
```

Column rule display : '-ah-column-rule-display'

■ Initial value: 'gap'   ■ Applies to: multi-column elements   ■ Inherited: no

A multi-column box might not have enough content to fill the number of column specified by 'columns', 'column-count', or 'column-width'. '-ah-column-rule-display' specifies whether to display a column rule between columns that would exist if the multi-column element contained sufficient content.

- 'gap' : Display a rule only between existing columns.
- 'end' : Display a rule at the end side of each existing column.
- 'all' : Display rules even between non-existent columns.

```
div.MultiCol3 {
    -ah-column-rule-display: end;
}
```

```
-ah-column-rule-          plays a rule after each
display:  end;  dis-      column.
```

KEEPS & BREAKS

Paged media is, obviously, divided into pages. CSS provides multiple properties for controlling whether the content of an element should be kept together on column or one page and whether there should or should not be a column or page break before or after the content. AH Formatter provides the '-ah-keep-together-within-dimension' property for finer control of the 'break-inside' property.

Controlling Breaks

Breaks between boxes : 'break-before' / 'page-break-after'

■ Initial value: 'auto'   ■ Applies to: block elements   ■ Inherited: no

These properties specify page or column break behavior . 'left', 'right', 'page', and 'column' values create a forced break in the flow while 'avoid', 'avoid-page' and 'avoid-column' values indicate that content should be kept together.

- 'auto' : Neither force nor forbid a break.
- 'always' : Always force a break before or after the principal box.
- 'avoid' : Avoid a break before or after the principal box.
- 'page' : Force a page break before or after the principal box.
- 'column' : Force a column break before or after the principal box.
- 'avoid-page' : Avoid a page break before or after the principal box.
- 'avoid-column' : Avoid a column break before or after the principal box.
- 'left' : Force one or two page breaks so the next page is a left-hand page.
- 'right' : Force one or two page breaks so the next page is a right-hand page.

Breaks within boxes : 'break-inside'

■ Initial value: 'auto'   ■ Applies to: block elements   ■ Inherited: no

This property specifies page or column break behavior within the element's principal box.

- 'auto' : Impose no additional constraints.
- 'avoid' : Avoid breaks within the box.
- 'avoid-page' : Avoid page breaks within the box.
- 'avoid-column' : Avoid column breaks within the box.

Limiting effect of 'break-inside' : '-ah-keep-together-within-dimension'

◼ Initial value: 'all'   ◼ Applies to: block elements   ◼ Inherited: no

This property specifies the height of a box for which a non-auto 'break-inside' property value is effective. Above that height, 'break-inside' behaves as if 'auto' was specified.

- 'all' : No restriction on effect of 'break-inside' property.
- <length> : Upper limit of the height of a box for which a non-auto 'break-inside' property value is effective.

```
.BigBlock {
  /* Keep the block together, but allow it to break if
     it exceeds the height of the page. */
  break-inside: avoid;
  -ah-keep-together-within-dimension: 100vh;
}
```

Control of Page Breaks

Page break : 'page-break-before' / 'page-break-after'

◼ Initial value: 'auto'   ◼ Applies to: block elements   ◼ Inherited: no

- 'auto' : Neither force nor forbid a page break.
- 'always' : Always force a page break.
- 'avoid' : Avoid a page break.
- 'left' : Force one or two page breaks so the next page is a left-hand page.
- 'right' : Force one or two page breaks so the next page is a right-hand page.

```
/* forced page break before top header (h1) */
h1 {
  page-break-before: always;
}
```

```
/* insert break page after this block */
div.Ending {
  page-break-after: always;
}
```

Setting either property's value to 'avoid' prohibit a page break either before or after the specified element.

```
/* Avoid page breaks immediate after headings (h1-h6) */
h1, h2, h3, h4, h5, h6 {
  page-break-after: avoid;
}
```

6

Pages starting from either the left or right

The first page of a chapter can be set to start either on the right or left. Blank pages are inserted if necessary.

```css
/* Insert page break so that h2 is always kept on the right. */
h2 {
  page-break-before: right;
}
```

Prohibit page break : 'page-break-inside'

■ Initial value: 'auto' ■ Applies to: block elements ■ Inherited: yes

Setting the value to avoid, prohibits page breaks within the specified element.

- 'auto' : Neither force nor forbid a page break.
- 'avoid' : Avoid a page break.

```css
/* Avoid page breaks in this block */
div.NoBreak {
  page-break-inside: avoid;
}
```

Minimum Lines Before Or After A Page Break : 'orphans'/'widows'

■ Initial value: 2 ■ Applies to: block elements ■ Inherited: yes

'orphans' specifies the minimum number of lines of a paragraph that must be left at the bottom of a page. 'widows' specifies the minimum number of lines that must be left at the top of a page.

- <integer> : Minimum number of lines before or after a page break.

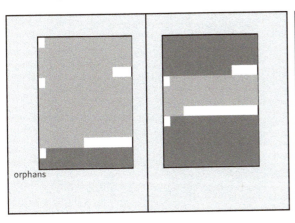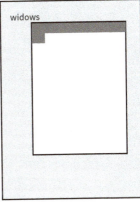

Orphan and widow lines

6

PARAGRAPH SETTING

The lines with a block of text, such as for a paragraph, may be aligned to one side or another or aligned to both. If the text within the lines has varying font sizes or alignment baselines, then line spacing can become irregular. AH Formatter provides extension properties for maintaining consistent line spacing both within and across blocks. If words at the ends of lines in justified text are allowed to be hyphenated, this can reduce the amount of white-space within the lines.

Alignment

Text alignment : 'text-align'

■ Initial value: depends on characters display direction   ■ Applies to: block elements   ■ Inherited: yes

Aligns the lines of text to the left, right, or center or justifies the text.

'left' : Content is aligned to the left.

AH Formatter provides features for optimal formatting, including: custom-developed MathML 3, CGM, and SVG rendering; baseline grids; PANTONE® spot colors; and properties for controlling Japanese layout.

'right' : Content is aligned to the right.

AH Formatter provides features for optimal formatting, including: custom-developed MathML 3, CGM, and SVG rendering; baseline grids; PANTONE® spot colors; and properties for controlling Japanese layout.

'center' : Content is centered within the line box.

AH Formatter provides features for optimal formatting, including: custom-developed MathML 3, CGM, and SVG rendering; baseline grids; PANTONE® spot colors; and properties for controlling Japanese layout.

7

'inside' : Content is aligned to the gutter side of the line box.

AH Formatter provides features for optimal formatting, including: custom-developed MathML 3, CGM, and SVG rendering; baseline grids; PANTONE® spot colors; and properties for controlling Japanese layout.

'outside' : Content is aligned to the fore-edge side of the line box.

AH Formatter provides features for optimal formatting, including: custom-developed MathML 3, CGM, and SVG rendering; baseline grids; PANTONE® spot colors; and properties for controlling Japanese layout.

'start' : Content is aligned to the start edge of the line box.

AH Formatter provides features for optimal formatting, including: custom-developed MathML 3, CGM, and SVG rendering; baseline grids; PANTONE® spot colors; and properties for controlling Japanese layout.

'end' : Content is aligned to the end edge of the line box.

AH Formatter provides features for optimal formatting, including: custom-developed MathML 3, CGM, and SVG rendering; baseline grids; PANTONE® spot colors; and properties for controlling Japanese layout.

'justify' : Content is justified to fill the line box.

AH Formatter provides features for optimal formatting, including: custom-developed MathML 3, CGM, and SVG rendering; baseline grids; PANTONE® spot colors; and properties for controlling Japanese layout.

<string> : Table cell content is aligned on a string.

AH Formatter provides an extension to 'text-align' that applies only in table cells. Specifying a string aligns the cell contents on the specified string. For example, `text-align: ".";` on every cell in a column will align a column of numbers on the decimal point. See Horizontal Alignment in Table Cells (page 79).

Year	Q1	Q2	Q3	Q4
2016	9.1	1.25	6	3.69
2017	1.74	9	5.55	2.1
2018	12.1	3.78	4.1	0

The 'text-align' property 'start' and 'end' values are extended from CSS 3. When `text-align: start;` or `text-align: end;` is specified for vertical text, the text is aligned to the top or bottom.

'end': content is aligned to the end edge

親譲りの無鉄砲で小供の時から損ばかりしている。小学校に居る時分学校の二階から飛び降りて一週間ほど腰を抜かした事がある。なぜそんな無闇をしたと聞く人があるかも知れぬ。別段深い理由でもない。

'start': content is aligned to the start edge

親譲りの無鉄砲で小供の時から損ばかりしている。小学校に居る時分学校の二階から飛び降りて一週間ほど腰を抜かした事がある。なぜそんな無闇をしたと聞く人があるかも知れぬ。別段深い理由でもない。

Alignment of the last line : 'text-align-last' 🄴

■ Initial value: 'start' ■ Applies to: all elements ■ Inherited: yes

'text-align-last' specifies the alignment of just the last line of a block or a line right before a forced line break.

`text-align-last: left;` (aligned to the left)

AH Formatter provides features for optimal formatting, including: custom-developed MathML 3, CGM, and SVG rendering; baseline grids; PANTONE® spot colors; and properties for controlling Japanese layout.

`text-align-last: right;` (aligned to the right)

AH Formatter provides features for optimal formatting, including: custom-developed MathML 3, CGM, and SVG rendering; baseline grids; PANTONE® spot colors; and properties for controlling Japanese layout.

`text-align-last: center;` (aligned to the center)

AH Formatter provides features for optimal formatting, including: custom-developed MathML 3, CGM, and SVG rendering; baseline grids; PANTONE® spot colors; and properties for controlling Japanese layout.

`text-align-last: inside;` (aligned to the gutter)

AH Formatter provides features for optimal formatting, including: custom-developed MathML 3, CGM, and SVG rendering; baseline grids; PANTONE® spot colors; and properties for controlling Japanese layout.

7

`text-align-last: outside;` (aligned to the fore-edge)

AH Formatter provides features for optimal formatting, including: custom-developed MathML 3, CGM, and SVG rendering; baseline grids; PANTONE® spot colors; and properties for controlling Japanese layout.

`text-align-last: start;` (aligned to the start edge)

AH Formatter provides features for optimal formatting, including: custom-developed MathML 3, CGM, and SVG rendering; baseline grids; PANTONE® spot colors; and properties for controlling Japanese layout.

`text-align-last: end;` (aligned to the end edge)

AH Formatter provides features for optimal formatting, including: custom-developed MathML 3, CGM, and SVG rendering; baseline grids; PANTONE® spot colors;
and properties for controlling Japanese layout.

`text-align-last: justify;` (aligned to both ends)

AH Formatter provides features for optimal formatting, including: custom-developed MathML 3, CGM, and SVG rendering; baseline grids; PANTONE® spot colors;
and   properties   for   controlling   Japanese   layout.

`text-align-last: end;` (aligned to end edge)

親譲りの無鉄砲で小供の時から損ばかりしている。小学校に居る時分学校の二階から飛び降りて一週間ほど腰を抜かした事がある。なぜそんな無闇をしたと聞く人があるかも知れぬ。別段深い理由でもない。

`text-align-last: start;` (aligned to start edge)

親譲りの無鉄砲で小供の時から損ばかりしている。小学校に居る時分学校の二階から飛び降りて一週間ほど腰を抜かした事がある。なぜそんな無闇をしたと聞く人があるかも知れぬ。別段深い理由でもない。

Alignment of the first line : 'text-align-first' property

■ Initial value: 'relative' ■ Applies to: all elements ■ Inherited: yes

'text-align-first' specifies the alignment of the first line of a block and of a line immediately after a forced line break. For a one-line block, 'text-align-first' (if not 'relative') has precedence over 'text-align-last'.

- 'relative' : Does nothing.

- 'start' : Content is aligned to the start edge.
- 'end' : Content is aligned to the end edge.
- 'center' : Content is aligned to the center.
- 'inside' : Content is aligned to the gutter edge.
- 'outside' : Content is aligned to the fore-edge edge.
- 'justify' : Content is aligned to both the start and end edges.
- 'left' : Content is aligned to the left edge.
- 'right' : Content is aligned to the right edge.

Line height with superscripts or subscripts : '-ah-line-height-shift-adjustment' 🔲

🔲 Initial value: consider-shifts 🔲 Applies to: inline-level elements 🔲 Inherited: yes

Line stacking can be irregular when lines contain superscripts and subscripts. Specify `-ah-line-height-shift-adjustment: disregard-shifts` to stop superscripts and subscripts from influencing the line stacking. However, line stacking can still change for images, fonts with different character baseline positions (such as mixed Japanese and European text), and large letters.

- 'consider-shifts' : Shifted position of characters is used for determining line-height.
- 'disregard-shifts' : Unshifted position of characters is used for determining line-height.

Without `-ah-line-height-shift-adjustment: disregard-shifts;`

Line stacking can be irregular when lines contain superscripts [ABC] and subscripts [abc]. Specify `-ah-line-height-shift-adjustment: disregard-shifts` to stop superscripts and subscripts from influencing the line stacking. However, line stacking can still change for images, fonts with different character baseline positions (such as mixed Japanese and European text), and large letters.

With `-ah-line-height-shift-adjustment: disregard-shifts;`

Line stacking can be irregular when lines contain superscripts [ABC] and subscripts [abc]. Specify `-ah-line-height-shift-adjustment: disregard-shifts` to stop superscripts and subscripts from influencing the line stacking. However, line stacking can still change for images, fonts with different character baseline positions (such as mixed Japanese and European text), and large letters.

7

Line stacking : '-ah-line-stacking-strategy' ◪

■ Initial value: line-height ■ Applies to: block elements ■ Inherited: yes

When a line contains a mixture of large letters, superscripts and subscripts, and images, or fonts with different character baseline positions (such as mixed Japanese and European text), line stacking depends on the characters that each line contains. As a result, line stacking becomes irregular. Specifying `-ah-line-stacking-strategy: font-height;` will make line stacking uniform.

- 'line-height' : CSS-style line box stacking with half-leading included in line-area.
- 'font-height' : Line-area is based on font of block-area; equal baseline-to-baseline spacing.
- 'max-height' : Line-area is minimum required to enclose inline areas; constant space between line-areas.

Without `-ah-line-stacking-strategy: font-height;`

When a line contains a mixture of large letters, superscripts ABC and subscripts abc, and images, or fonts with different character baseline positions (such as mixed Japanese and European text), line stacking depends on the characters that each line contains. As a result, line stacking becomes irregular. Specifying `-ah-line-stacking-strategy: font-height;` will make line stacking uniform.

With `-ah-line-stacking-strategy: font-height;`

When a line contains a mixture of large letters, superscripts ABC and subscripts abc, and images, or fonts with different character baseline positions (such as mixed Japanese and European text), line stacking depends on the characters that each line contains. As a result, line stacking can become irregular. Specifying `-ah-line-stacking-strategy: font-height;` will make line stacking uniform.

Baseline grid[6]

'-ah-line-stacking-strategy' affects the lines within a single block. It does not, however, the lines of multiple blocks. Line areas across multiple blocks can be aligned to a consistent line spacing by using the '-ah-baseline-grid' property.

Some line areas, however, will not align with the baseline grid that is used for running text. These include:

- Headings are frequently in a larger font size than running text. It is sometimes possible to maintain consistent line spacing for running text by carefully setting the 'margin-top' and 'margin-bottom' of each level of heading so that each

---

6 The baseline grid feature is not available in AH Formatter Lite.

heading occupies the same height as an integral number of lines. However, that can fail when a heading extends over more than one line or a heading is immediately followed by another heading.

- Few graphics are exactly the same height as an integer number of lines.
- Borders and padding on table cells can affect the regular line spacing of table text.

Blocks that have content that does not fit with the baseline grid can have the entire block aligned with the grid by using the '-ah-baseline-block-snap' property.

Without baseline grid

Preamble

Whereas recognition of the inherent dignity and of the equal and inalienable rights of all members of the human family is the foundation of freedom, justice and peace in the world,

Whereas disregard and contempt for human rights have resulted in barbarous acts which have outraged the conscience of mankind, and the advent of

a world in which human beings shall enjoy freedom of speech and belief and freedom from fear and want has been proclaimed as the highest aspiration of the common people,

Whereas it is essential, if man is not to be compelled to have recourse, as a last resort, to rebellion against tyranny and oppression, that human rights should be protected by the rule of law,

With baseline grid

Preamble

Whereas recognition of the inherent dignity and of the equal and inalienable rights of all members of the human family is the foundation of freedom, justice and peace in the world,

Whereas disregard and contempt for human rights have resulted in barbarous acts which have outraged the conscience of mankind, and the advent of

a world in which human beings shall enjoy freedom of speech and belief and freedom from fear and want has been proclaimed as the highest aspiration of the common people,

Whereas it is essential, if man is not to be compelled to have recourse, as a last resort, to rebellion against tyranny and oppression, that human rights should be protected by the rule of law,

7

Setting the baseline grid : '-ah-baseline-grid'

■ Initial value: 'normal'　■ Applies to: block containers　■ Inherited: no

Sets or clears the baseline grid. The line areas that are within an area in which a baseline grid is set are aligned with baselines on the baseline grid.

- 'normal' : Neither sets nor clears the baseline grid.

- 'none' : Clears the baseline grid and the content will not align with a baseline grid.
- 'new' : Sets a new baseline grid.
- 'root' : Sets the baseline grid defined by the root element.

Aligning blocks to the baseline grid : '-ah-baseline-block-snap' ◪
■ Initial value: auto border-box ■ Applies to: block-level elements with `-ah-baseline-grid: new;` or `-ah-baseline-grid: none;` ■ Inherited: no

Specifies how to align blocks other than normal line boxes, such as headings, figures and tables, to the baseline grid.
- 'none' : block is not aligned with the baseline grid.
- 'auto' : at top of column, same as 'before'; at bottom of column, same as 'after'; otherwise 'center'.
- 'before' : before edge of the block is aligned with a text-before-edge baseline on the baseline grid.
- 'after' : after edge of the block is aligned with a text-after-edge baseline on the baseline grid.
- 'center' : block is centered between a text-before-edge and a text-after-edge baseline on the baseline grid.
- 'border-box' : border edge is used to align the block on the baseline grid.
- 'margin-box' : margin edge is used to align the block on the baseline grid.

'auto', 'before', 'after', or 'center' may be combined with either 'border-box' or 'margin-box'. 'none' may not be combined with any other value.

Leader : 'leader()' function ▤

With the 'leader()' function, a leader (such as dots) can be added, for example, between the title page and page number in the table of contents and align the page number to the right.

Any of the following may be used as leaders: dotted, solid, space, or characters.

- leader(dotted) . . . . leader(dotted)
- leader(solid) _____ leader(solid)
- leader(space)   leader(space)
- leader("*-") *- leader("*-")

Using space as a leader gives the effect of a right-aligned tab stop.

Quadratic formula $x = \dfrac{-b \pm \sqrt{b^2 - 4ac}}{2a}$ (1)

Hyphenation

AH Formatter provides an extension feature of hyphenation of more than forty languages. It uses language-specific algorithms so that you do not need to provide a hyphenation dictionary. If you want to hyphenate words that are not handled by the algorithms, you can add them to the exception dictionary.

Soft hyphens (U+00AD) can be explicitly inserted inside a word to allow hyphenation. In HTML, ­ represents the soft hyphen character. For example, "abcde" does not break, but a­b­c­d­e may be hyphenated: a-bcde.

To stop line breaks at literal hyphens, replace the hyphens with U+2011 NON-BREAKING HYPHEN (‑).

AH Formatter implements the 'hyphens' property defined in CSS 3 plus, among others, the 'hyphenate-before', 'hyphenate-after', and 'hyphenate-lines' that were defined in a previous GCPM Working Draft but have since been removed.

Hyphenation : 'hyphens' property 🗐
■ Initial value: 'manual'　■ Applies to: all elements　■ Inherited: yes

Set the 'hyphens' property to 'auto' to enable hyphenation. The hyphenation process uses a language-specific hyphenation algorithm to perform hyphenation for each language.

- 'none' : Disable both automatic hyphenation and hyphenation at soft hyphens.
- 'manual' : Disable automatic hyphenation and enable hyphenation at soft hyphens.
- 'auto' : Enable both automatic hyphenation and hyphenation at soft hyphens.

In these examples, lang specifies the language of the text:

```
.Hyphenated {
  hyphens: auto;
}
```

```
<div class="Hyphenated" lang="en">
  <p>Set the 'hyphens' property to 'auto' to …
```

Set the 'hyphens' property to 'auto' to enable hyphenation. The hyphenation process uses a language-specific hyphenation algorithm to perform hyphenation for each language.

```
<div lang="en">
  <p>Set the 'hyphens' property to 'auto' to …
```

7

> Set the 'hyphens' property to 'auto' to enable hyphenation. The hyphenation process uses a language- specific hyphenation algorithm to perform hyphenation for each language.

When hyphenation is enabled for body text, it is usually a good idea to disable it in headings and possibly also in other contexts where added hyphens could detract from the appearance of the text. For example, in captions, table headers, or even all table text.

```css
body:lang(en) {
  hyphens: auto;
}

h1, h2, h3, h4, h5, h6 {
  hyphens: manual;
}
```

Minimum number of characters : 'hyphenate-before'

■ Initial value: 'auto'   ■ Applies to: all elements   ■ Inherited: yes

Specifies the minimum number of characters in a hyphenated word before the hyphenation character with a default value of 2, but this can be adjusted in the AH Formatter Option Setting File.

For example, the six-letter word 'hyphen' can be hyphenated as 'hy-phen'. If `hyphenate-before: 3;` is specified, the number of characters before the word break is less than three letters, so the word 'hyphen' is not hyphenated.

Minimum number of characters : 'hyphenate-after'

■ Initial value: 'auto'   ■ Applies to: all elements   ■ Inherited: yes

Specifies the minimum number of characters in a hyphenated word after the hyphenation character with a default value of 2, but this can be adjusted in the AH Formatter Option Setting File.

For example, the six-letter word 'hyphen' can be hyphenated as 'hy-phen'. If `hyphenate-after: 5;` is specified, the number of characters after the word break is less than five letters, so the word 'hyphen' is not hyphenated.

Maximum number of hyphenated lines : 'hyphenate-lines'

■ Initial value: 'no-limit'   ■ Applies to: all elements   ■ Inherited: yes

Specifies the maximum number of consecutive lines in an element that end with a hyphenated word.

- 'no-limit' : No limit to the number of consecutive lines.
- <integer> : Maximum number of consecutive lines.

Progression Direction : 'writing-mode' 🔲

■ Initial value: 'lr-tb'　■ Applies to: all elements　■ Inherited: yes

　　Specify 'writing-mode' on the root element to set the character, line, and page progression direction of the entire document. The Initial value is `writing-mode: lr-tb;` (left-to-right, top-to-bottom): the character progression direction is from left to right, the line and block progression directions are from top to bottom, and the pages go from left to right[7].

　　To set documents in Japanese vertical writing mode, specify `writing-mode: tb-rl;`. The character progression direction is from top-to-bottom, line and block from right-to-left, and pages from right to left.

- 'lr-tb' : Writing mode progression direction is from left to right, the line and block from top to bottom. Used in conventional horizontal writing.
- 'rl-tb' : Writing mode progression direction is from right to left, the line and block from top to bottom. Used in right-to-left languages such as Arabic and Hebrew.
- 'tb-rl' : Writing mode progression direction is from top to bottom, the line and block from right to left. Used in vertical writing such as Japanese.

　　Specifying `writing-mode: tb-rl;` on the block element sets vertical writing orientation for the block. In block vertical writing, the page progression direction remains left to right as in horizontal writing.

```
div.VerticalTextBlock {
    writing-mode: tb-rl;      /* vertical writing */
    height: 16em;             /* number of characters in a line */
    padding: 3pt; border: ridge green;
}
```

7

---

7 The writing-mode on the root element is inherited by the page box, and is then inherited by the margin box.

日本語は伝統的に縦書きで組まれます。書籍や雑誌など、出版物の多くは今も縦書きが主流です。AH CSS Formatter は縦書きにも対応してこのように、部分的にブロックを縦書きにすることも、文書全体を縦書きにもできます。

縦書きの指定は writing-mode: tb-rl です。tb-rl は、文字の進行方向が上から下 (top-to-bottom)、行とブロックの進行方向が右から左 (right-to-left) を意味しています。

横書きの指定は writing-mode: lr-tb (left-to-right and top-to-bottom) です。アラビア語やヘブライ語などの右から左に書く言語の横書きの場合は writing-mode: rl-tb (right-to-left, top-to-bottom) です。

縦書きの中に「'08年12月8日」のように部分的に数字などを横書きにすることを「縦中横」といいます。

7

FOOTNOTES & SIDENOTES

Footnotes and sidenotes are used for (typically short) notes that are associated with a point in the main text. In the HTML or XML markup, the content of the note is included at that point in the main text.

There are four aspects to formatting a note as a footnote or sidenote:

- Moving of the note out of the main flow.
- Positioning of the note. For a footnote, this is typically but not always at the foot of the current page (or of a following page). For a sidenote, this is typically in the page margin.
- Leaving a marker behind in the main text.
- Generating a marker alongside the note in its position outside of the main text flow.

The two markers are typically the same text, although they will often differ in size or alignment baseline or in their added punctuation.

Footnote Setting : `float: footnote`

When `float: footnote;` is specified, [1].

```
.Footnote {
  float: footnote;
}
```

```
<p>When <span class="code">float: footnote;</span> is specified,
<span class="Footnote">the contents of the element will become a
footnote</span>.</p>
```

Use a '@footnote' rule in the '@page' rule to style the footnote area. Use `float: page bottom;` (see Page float : float: top page / float: bottom page (page 111)) to arrange footnotes at the bottom of the page. Use the pseudo-elements '::footnote-call' and '::footnote-marker' to set the footnote marker format.

8

---

1 the contents of the element will become a footnote

Footnote Style : '@footnote' rule ⊟

Use the '@footnote' rule in the '@page' rule to style the footnote area, for example, by drawing a ruled line above the footnote area.

```
@page {
  @footnote {
    float: bottom page; /* The footnote area is placed as a float at
                           the bottom of the page */
    border-top: thin solid black; /* Set a ruled line above the
                                     footnote area */
    border-length: 30%;          /* Line length is 30% of
                                    the page area width */
    padding-top: 0.5em;
  }
}
```

Footnote Number : '::footnote-call'/ '::footnote-marker' pseudo-elements ⊟

Use '::footnote-call' and '::footnote-marker' to set the footnote number. The "footnote" counter is incremented each time that a footnote is generated.[2]

```
::footnote-call {    /* footnote call */
  content: counter(footnote) ")";
  font-size: 6pt;
  vertical-align: super;
}
::footnote-marker { /* footnote number */
  content: counter(footnote) ")";
  font-size: 1em;
  vertical-align: super;
}
```

8 Length of footnote separator : 'border-length' ⊟

■ Initial value: 'auto'　■ Applies to: '@footnote' areas　■ Inherited: no

The 'border-length' property specifies the length of the border between footnotes and other content. If the length of the border between the areas is longer than the 'border-length' value, then part of the border will be transparent and the background of the footnote area will be shown instead.

- • 'auto' : Full-width border.
- • <length> : Length of the border. Percentages refer to the normal length of the border.

---

2 As you can see from the marker for this footnote

Sidenote Setting : `float: sidenote` 🗐

When `float: sidenote;` is specified for the 'float' property, the contents will become a sidenote. Use the '@sidenote' rule in the '@page' rule to set the sidenote area. Use the pseudo-elements '::sidenote-call' and '::sidenote-marker' to set the sidenote number format.

```
span.sidenote {
  float: sidenote;
}
```

> Whereas recognition of the inherent dignity[1] and of the equal and
> inalienable rights of all members of the human family is the foun-
> dation of freedom, justice and peace in the world,
>
> [1] This is a sidenote.

Sidenote Style : '@sidenote' rule 🗐

Use the '@sidenote' rule in the '@page' rule to set the position and extent of a sidenote area.

```
@page {
  @sidenote {
    float: outside;
    clear: both;
    width: 20%;
  }
}
```

TABLES

The CSS table model is based on the HTML4 table model. Tables should be used only for content with logical row and/or column relationships. Elements that are displayed as tables will be tagged as tables in Tagged PDF and PDF/UA output. As such, if the elements are not logically a table, they will be confusing to a user of assistive technologies.

How to Create Tables

When using CSS with a document language that does not have table elements, you can map document elements to 'display' property values that correspond to the HTML4 table elements.

'display' Value	HTML Element
'table'	TABLE
'inline-table'	TABLE
'table-row'	TR
'table-row-group'	TBODY
'table-header-group'	THEAD
'table-footer-group'	TFOOT
'table-column'	COL
'table-column-group'	COLGROUP
'table-cell'	TD, TH
'table-caption'	CAPTION

Mapping elements to table-related 'display' values is so generally useful that CSS style sheets for HTML (such as html.css that is distributed with AH Formatter) map

HTML table elements to the 'display' values that are defined to display like that same element:

```
table        { display: table }
tr           { display: table-row }
thead        { display: table-header-group }
tbody        { display: table-row-group }
tfoot        { display: table-footer-group }
col          { display: table-column }
colgroup     { display: table-column-group }
td, th       { display: table-cell }
caption      { display: table-caption }
```

You can display your XML as a table by associating XML elements with the 'display' property values that represent table elements.

```
<DATA>
  <STACK>
    <ROW><CELL>row 1 column 1</CELL><CELL>row 1 column 2</CELL></ROW>
    <ROW><CELL>row 2 column 1</CELL></ROW>
    <ROW><CELL>row 3 column 1</CELL></ROW>
  </STACK>
</DATA>
```

```
DATA {
  display: block;
  margin: 20%;
}
STACK {
  display: table;
  border-collapse: collapse;
}
ROW  {
  display: table-row;
}
CELL {
  display: table-cell;
  padding: 10pt;
  font-weight: bolder;
  border: solid thin;
}
```

9

row 1 column 1	row 1 column 2
row 2 column 1	
row 3 column 1	

XML displayed as table

Properties That Apply To Table Elements

Ordinarily, the 'margin', 'border', 'padding', 'width', and 'height' properties of a CSS box determine its dimensions. Tables are slightly different, since some of the properties do not apply to every table-related box.

Properties that apply to table elements

'display' Value	'margin'	'border'	'padding'	'width'	'height'
'table'	yes	yes	yes	yes	yes
'inline-table'	yes	yes	yes	yes	yes
'table-row'	no	yes	no	no	yes
'table-row-group'	no	yes	no	no	yes
'table-header-group'	no	yes	no	yes	yes
'table-footer-group'	no	yes	no	yes	yes
'table-column'	no	yes	no	yes	no
'table-column-group'	no	yes	no	yes	no
'table-cell'	no	yes	yes	yes	yes
'table-caption'	yes	yes	yes	yes	yes

▪ Table padding applies only when `border-collapse: separate;`

9

- When `border-collapse: separate;`, the width of a table is the length between the inner side of the left and right padding. When `border-collapse: collapse;`, the width is the length between the center of the left and right borders.
- Border properties on 'table-column', 'table-column-group', 'table-row', and 'table-row-group' apply only when `border-collapse: collapse;`.
- The 'width' property values of 'table-column' and 'table-column-group' specify the minimum width of a column.

Table Border Model

Whether to merge adjacent borders : 'border-collapse'

■ Initial value: 'separate'   ■ Applies to: 'table' elements   ■ Inherited: yes
Specifies whether to treat the borders around each CSS table cell individually.
- 'collapse' : Merge the borders of adjacent cells.
- 'separate' : Treat borders of adjacent cells separately.

Spaces between borders : 'border-spacing'

■ Initial value: 0px 0px   ■ Applies to: 'table' and 'inline-table' elements
■ Inherited: yes
Specifies the space (white space) between the borders of adjacent cells when `border-collapse: separate;`.
- <length>{1,2} : Distance that separates adjoining cell borders. If one length is specified, it gives both the horizontal and vertical spacing. If two are specified, the first gives the horizontal spacing and the second the vertical spacing.

```
table {
    padding: 5mm;
    border: solid 2mm gray;
    border-collapse: separate;
    border-spacing: 2mm;
}

th, td {
    padding: 2mm;
    border: solid 2mm silver;
}
```

9

An example of the above specification is as follows:

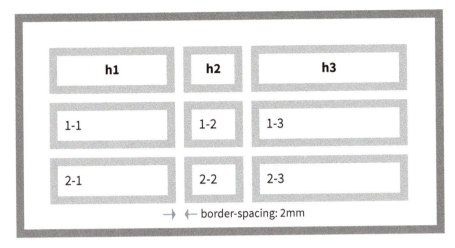

→ ← border-spacing: 2mm

Table with `border-collapse: separate;`

```
table {
  padding: 5mm;
  border: solid 2mm gray;
  border-collapse: collapse;
}

th, td {
  padding: 2mm;
  border: solid 2mm silver;
}
```

An example of the above specification follows. This time, the table padding disappears. Since the table and cell borders are the same width and style, their priority is determined by the 'display' value, so the border of the box generated by table is overwritten by the cell border.

h1	h2	h3
1-1	1-2	1-3
2-1	2-2	2-3

Table with `border-collapse: collapse;`

9

Border priority

As in the previous example, `border-collapse: collapse;` combines the adjacent borders together. The priority of the borders is as follows:

- `border-style: hidden;` has the highest priority.
- `border-style: none;` has the lowest priority.
- Wide borders have higher priority than narrow borders.
- Borders with the same width are prioritized according to the style of the border in descending order as follows:
  1. 'double'
  2. 'solid'
  3. 'dashed'
  4. 'dotted'
  5. 'ridge'
  6. 'outset'
  7. 'groove'
  8. 'inset'

  'double' has the highest priority, and 'inset' has the lowest.
- Borders differing only in color are prioritized according to the 'display' type of the element in descending order as follows:
  1. 'table-cell'
  2. 'table-row'
  3. 'table-row-group'
  4. 'table-column'
  5. 'table-column-group'
  6. 'table'

  'table' has the lowest priority.
- In horizontal, left-to-right writing, if the element types are the same and have line types of the same property, the further it is to the left, the higher its priority. In horizontal, right-to-left writing, the further to the right it is, the higher the priority.

Determining Table and Column Width : 'table-layout'

■ Initial value: 'auto'   ■ Applies to: 'table' elements   ■ Inherited: no

Specifying 'table-layout' property determines the width of the table columns.

- 'auto' : Automatically calculates the width of table columns and lays out the table.
- 'fixed' : Lays out tables based on the fixed values of table and column widths.

When the value is 'auto', table width depends on its content. The minimum width of a column can be specified by the 'width' property of the column element[1], but

---

1 Equivalent to HTML `col` element

the program automatically determines the width for other columns from the cell contents and the width of the entire table.

`table-layout: fixed;` determines the width of the table and does not depend on the contents of the cells. If the width of the table is not specified, then the width of table is the width of the block that contains the table. The width of each column is determined as follows:

- If the column width is specified by the 'width' property value of the corresponding `<column>` element, that column has the same value.
- Otherwise, the 'width' property value of the cell in the first row sets the column width.
- The remaining width, (width of the entire table minus the specified column widths) is evenly allocated to any remaining columns.

```
table {
  table-layout: fixed;
  ...
}

col.first {
  width: 10em;
}
```

Align Table to Center

Specify `margin-left: auto;` and `margin-right: auto;` to center the entire table.

```
table {
  margin-left: auto;
  margin-right: auto;
  ...
}
```

Table Caption Position : 'caption-side'

■ Initial value: 'top'　■ Applies to: 'caption' elements　■ Inherited: yes

Use the 'caption-side' property to specify the position of the table caption.

- 'top' : Displays the caption above the table.
- 'bottom' : Displays the caption below the table.

```
table {
  caption-side: top;
  ...
}
```

9

Caption positioned above the table

Product Introduction	
Option name	**Product content**
SVG option	This is an option for SVG output.
Barcode option	Provides several style sheets for printing barcodes and barcode fonts.

```
table {
    caption-side: bottom;
    ...
}
```

Caption positioned below the table

Option name	**Product content**
SVG option	This is an option for SVG output.
Barcode option	Provides several style sheets for printing barcodes and barcode fonts.
Product Introduction	

Table Header and Footer

The table header is rendered at the top of the table, and the table footer is rendered at the bottom.

Table header and footer

Header	Header
R1C1	R1C2
R2C1	R2C2
R3C1	R3C2
R4C1	R4C2
Footer	**Footer**

When a table is split across a column or page, the default behavior is to render the table footer at the bottom of each part and render the table header at the top of each part.

9

Table header and footer repeated at break

Header	Header
R1C1	R1C2
R2C1	R2C2
Footer	Footer

Header	Header
R3C1	R3C2
R4C1	R4C2
Footer	Footer

Table header and footer at breaks : '-ah-table-omit-header-at-break'/'-ah-table-omit-footer-at-break' 🔲

■ Initial value: 'false'   ■ Applies to: 'table' and 'inline-table' elements
■ Inherited: no

These properties specify whether the table header or footer should be omitted when the table breaks across a column or page.

- 'false' : Do not omit the header or footer.
- 'true' : Omit the header or footer at both column and page breaks.
- 'column' : Omit the header or footer at column breaks but not at page breaks.[2]

Table header and footer omitted at break

Header	Header
R1C1	R1C2
R2C1	R2C2

R3C1	R3C2
R4C1	R4C2
Footer	Footer

Horizontal Alignment in Table Cells

The 'text-align' property for specifying horizontal alignment applies to table cells. AH Formatter provides an extension to 'text-align' that applies only in table cells for aligning the cell contents on a specified string. For example, `text-align: ".";` on every cell in a column will align a column of numbers on the decimal point.

AH Formatter also provides the '-ah-text-align-string' property for the overall alignment of a column of cells that are each aligned on a string.

Overall alignment when aligned on a character : '-ah-text-align-string' 🔲

■ Initial value: 'end'   ■ Applies to: table cell elements   ■ Inherited: yes

'-ah-text-align-string' specifies the overall alignment of the text in a table cell when the 'text-align' property value is a string. The allowed values are a subset of the values of 'text-align':

- 'start' : Align to the start edge.
- 'center' : Align to the center.

9

___
2 This feature is not available in AH Formatter Lite.

- 'end' : Align to the end edge.
- 'inside' : Align to the inside edge.
- 'outside' : Align to the outside edge.
- 'left' : Align to the left edge.
- 'right' : Align to the right edge.

The same '-ah-text-align-string' value should be used for all table cells within one column that are aligned on a string. Different values may be used on different cells within one column, but the result is likely to be confusing for the reader.

'-ah-text-align-string' values with `text-align: ".";`

'start'	'center'	'end'	'inside'	'outside'	'left'	'right'
1	1	1	1	1	1	1
1.0	1.0	1.0	1.0	1.0	1.0	1.0
1.00	1.00	1.00	1.00	1.00	1.00	1.00
123	123	123	123	123	123	123
12.3	12.3	12.3	12.3	12.3	12.3	12.3

Vertical Alignment in Table Cells

A subset of the 'vertical-align' property values apply to table cells, but with different meanings:

- 'baseline' : Baseline of the cell is aligned with the baseline of the first row that it spans.
- 'top' : Top of the cell box is aligned with the top of the first row that it spans.
- 'middle' : Center of the cell is aligned with the center of the rows that is spans.
- 'bottom' : Bottom of the cell is aligned with the bottom of the last row it spans.

All other 'vertical-align' values are ignored, and 'baseline' is used instead.

Cell and row baselines

The baseline of a table cell is the baseline of the first line box rendered in the cell (or the baseline of the first table row rendered in the cell, if that comes first). Otherwise, the baseline is the bottom content edge of the cell box.

The baseline of a table row is the maximum of the baselines of all of the cells in the row that have `vertical-align: baseline;` and for which the row is the first row that the cell spans.

9

Repeat Cell Content at Break : '-ah-repeat-cell-content-at-break'

Initial value: 'false'   Applies to: 'table-cell' elements   Inherited: no

If a table cell breaks across a page or column because another cell in the current row or the rows that the cell spans exceeds the available space but the contents of the cell fits within the first fragment, then the cell contents does not repeat after the break. When `-ah-repeat-cell-content-at-break: true;` is specified, the contents is repeated after the break.

- 'false' : Do not copy the contents of the cell.
- 'true' : Repeat the contents of the cell.

Cell content not repeated at break

Header	Header		Header	Header
R1-R4 C1	R1 C2			R3 C2
	R2 C2			R4 C2

Cell content repeated at break

Header	Header		Header	Header
R1-R4 C1	R1 C2		R1-R4 C1	R3 C2
	R2 C2			R4 C2

9

LISTS

The 'display' property does not have a value that will cause an element display as a list. However, `display: list-item;` does cause an element to generate a list item. Every list item has a marker, which is the bullet, number, or other mark that identifies the list item. In CSS 2, the formatting of the marker is specified using the the 'list-style-type', 'list-style-image', 'list-style-position', and 'list-style' properties. CSS 3 adds the '::marker' pseudo-element so that the list item marker can be styled with the full range of CSS properties and values. The 'list-style-type' and 'list-style-image' properties set the default contents of the '::marker' pseudo-element.

List Item Marker Image : 'list-style-image'

■ Initial value: 'none' ■ Applies to: list items ■ Inherited: yes

Specifies an image to use as the default contents of the list item marker. If 'list-style-image' is 'none' or the image is invalid, the default contents are given by 'list-style-type' instead.

- 'none' : No image.
- <image> : Image to use as the default contents.

List Item Marker Type : 'list-style-type'

■ Initial value: 'disc' ■ Applies to: list items ■ Inherited: yes

Specifies the default contents of the list item marker when 'list-style-image' is 'none' or the image is invalid. Otherwise, it is ignored.

- 'none' : The default contents are 'none'.
- <counter-style> : The default contents are that counter style.
- <string> : The string is used as the default contents.

List Item Marker Position : 'list-style-position'

■ Initial value: 'outside' ■ Applies to: list items ■ Inherited: yes

'list-item-position' helps to control the position of the list item marker.
- 'inside' : The '::marker' pseudo-element is placed inline immediately before where the '::before' pseudo-element would be placed.

10

- 'outside' : As 'inside', plus the 'position' property on the marker computes to 'marker'.

List Item Marker Shorthand : 'list-style'

■ Initial value: see individual properties   ■ Applies to: list items   ■ Inherited: see individual properties

'list-style' is a shorthand for setting 'list-style-type', 'list-style-image', and 'list-style-position'.

```
ul.References li {
  list-style: check;
  line-height: 1.1;
}
```

List Item Marker : '::marker' pseudo-element 🄳

'::marker' can be styled with the full range of CSS properties and values. The default contents are defined by the 'list-style-image' and 'list-style-type' properties, but that can be overridden by setting the 'content' property of the '::marker'.

10

CHARACTER SETTING

As stated in Box Model (page 11), text is formatted into line boxes. The 'line-height' property sets the minimal height of the line box, and the multiple font-related properties select the visual representation of the text. The '@font-face' rule adds the ability to fetch and activate font resources instead of relying solely on the fonts installed on the system. Additional properties control, for example, the vertical alignment of the text and whether it has an underline or overline or is struck through.

Line Height : 'line-height'

■ Initial value: 'normal'   ■ Applies to: all elements   ■ Inherited: yes

Specifies the minimal height of the line box.

- 'normal' : A "reasonable" value. AH Formatter initially defaults to 1.2.[1]
- <length> : Length to use in calculation of the line box height.
- <number> : The line box height is this number multiplied by the font size of the element. Negative values are illegal.
- <percentage> : The line box height is this percentage multiplied by the font size of the element. Negative values are illegal.

If a number is specified, the line height is the value multiplied by the font size. If a value of 1.6 is specified, this is the same as specifying the line-height as 160% or 1.6em. However, when a numeric value is specified, it is the number and not the actual line height that is inherited. If a descendant element has a different font size, then the number is use to calculate that element's line height.

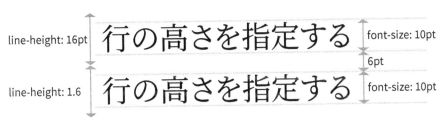

line-height: 16pt 行の高さを指定する font-size: 10pt

6pt

line-height: 1.6 行の高さを指定する font-size: 10pt

Line-height and space between lines

---

1 This value can be changed in the AH Formatter Option Setting File.

Font Properties

11

'font-family' and other font properties determine the font that is used to represent the text. A font 'face' (short for 'typeface') is a set of characters drawn with a particular style and with a common stroke weight, slant, or relative width. A font 'family' is a group of fonts sharing a common design style.

Font family : 'font-family'

■ Initial value: depends on user agent[2]   ■ Applies to: all elements
■ Inherited: yes

Specifies the type of font. May be a font name or keyword. The generic font family keywords are:

- 'sans-serif' : A plain font, such as Helvetica, that tends to have stroke endings with little or no ornamentation. A Gothic Japanese font is a sans-serif font.
- 'serif' : A font, such as Times, that tends to have a finishing stroke with flared or tapered ends. A Mincho Japanese font is a serif font.
- 'monospace' : A monospaced font. This is a font that has glyphs with the same fixed width.
- 'fantasy' : A decorative font.
- 'cursive' : A cursive font with either joining strokes or cursive characteristics.

If the font name contains spaces, such as "Times New Roman", enclose the name in double or single quotation marks.

Multiple fonts can be set separated by commas. Fonts available in the user environment are chosen in order of their appearance in the property value. AH Formatter identifies the script for each character or run of characters and selects the first listed font that supports that script. Japanese fonts support the Latin script and if, for example, you specify `font-family: "MS Gothic", Helvetica;`, this results in "MS Gothic" being used for the Latin script as well as Japanese[3]. Specifying a Latin font first, as shown in the following example, results in using Helvetica before MS Gothic.

```
font-family: Helvetica, "MS Gothic", sans-serif;
```

When a specific font might not be present on the system, it is advisable to include a generic font family, such as 'serif' or 'sans-serif', as the last font family in the list.

---

2 The initial value, 'serif', can be changed in the AH Formatter Option Setting File.
3 To select this font, the method of inspecting whether a font has glyphs for each single character has to change.

Font size : 'font-size'

■ Initial value: 'medium'   ■ Applies to: all elements   ■ Inherited: yes

Specifies the size of the font.

```css
/* Text */
body {
  font-size: 12pt;
  line-height: 1.5;
  font-family: Tahoma, "MS Gothic", sans-serif;
}
```

Font weight : 'font-weight'

■ Initial value: 'normal'   ■ Applies to: all elements   ■ Inherited: yes

Specifies the relative thickness or darkness of the strokes for the character.

- Assigned values : '100', '200', '300', '400', '500', '600', '700', '800', '900'. From '100', the thinnest and lightest, to '900', the thickest and darkest.
- 'normal' : standard (equivalent to 400).
- 'bold' : bold (equivalent to 700).
- 'lighter' : The next lighter font weight (subtracts 100).
- 'bolder' : The next darker font weight (adds 100).

When a weight is specified for which no face is available, a nearby weight is used.

Italic or Oblique type : 'font-style'

■ Initial value: 'normal'   ■ Applies to: all elements   ■ Inherited: yes

Specifies fonts as italic or oblique.

- 'normal' : standard ("upright").
- 'italic' : italic type
- 'oblique' : slanted

An 'italic' font is designed with a diagonal slant but 'oblique' is a normal font with a slant applied. If 'italic' is given but there is no italic type in the specified font, it will still display as a slanted font.

AH Formatter will treat characters as italic even if 'oblique' is specified.

There are practically no italic types in Japanese fonts, so even if italic or oblique is specified, it will display the same thing. Even in Japanese fonts, there are many fonts that have italics for alphabets.

font-style: italic;
CSS によるページ組版入門

font-style: oblique;
CSS によるページ組版入門

Italic and oblique styles for Japanese

Small capitals : 'font-variant'

■Initial value: 'normal' ■Applies to: all elements ■Inherited: yes

Use 'font-variant' to specify use of a small capitals font. AH Formatter will simulate the small capitals for a font does not include them.

- 'normal' : Sets all features to their initial values.
- 'none' : Disables ligatures and contextual alternates and resets all other features to their initial values.
- 'small-caps' : Use small capitals for lower-case letters.
- 'all-small-caps' : Use small capitals for upper-case and lower-case letters as well as for numbers and punctuation.

Small-caps variants

```
font-variant: normal;
```

Abc 123 &[]

```
font-variant: small-caps;
```

Abc 123 &[]

```
font-variant: all-small-caps;
```

ABC 123 &[]

Other font features

'font-variant' supports a large number of other keywords, such as 'oldstyle-nums', that correspond to OpenType features.

Setting 'font-variant' resets unspecified features to their initial values.

A font could implement only a subset of the OpenType features. AH Formatter will simulate the 'small-caps' and 'all-small-caps' features if the font does not support them. All other unsupported features will be ignored.

CSS3 defines 'font-variant' as a shorthand for multiple subproperties. AH Formatter does not implement the subproperties.

'font-variant' Keywords

normal | none | [<font-variant-caps> || <font-variant-numeric> || <font-variant-alternates> || <font-variant-ligatures> || <font-variant-position> || <font-variant-east-asian>]

Subset	Value
<font-variant-caps>	small-caps	all-small-caps	petite-caps	all-petite-caps	titling-caps	unicase
<font-variant-numeric>	<numeric-figure-values> || <numeric-spacing-values> || <numeric-fraction-values> || ordinal || slashed-zero
<numeric-figure-values>	lining-nums	oldstyle-nums
<numeric-spacing-values>	proportional-nums	tabular-nums
<numeric-fraction-values>	diagonal-fractions	stacked-fractions
<font-variant-alternates>	historical-forms	stylistic(<number>)	swash(<number>)	ornament(<number>)	annotation(<number>)	styleset(<number>#)	character-variant(<number>#)
<font-variant-ligatures>	<common-lig-values> || <discretionary-lig-values> || <historical-lig-values> || <contextual-alt-values>
<common-lig-values>	common-ligatures	no-common-ligatures
<discretionary-lig-values>	discretionary-ligatures	no-discretionary-ligatures
<historical-lig-values>	historical-ligatures	no-historical-ligatures
<contextual-alt-values>	contextual	no-contextual
<font-variant-position>	sub	super
<font-variant-east-asian>	<east-asian-variant-values> || <east-asian-width-values> || ruby
<east-asian-variant-values>	jis78	jis83	jis90	jis04	hojo-kanji	nlckanji	simplified	traditional
<east-asian-width-values>	full-width	half-width	third-width	quarter-width	proportional-width

Font : 'font'

■ Initial value: see individual properties ■ Applies to: all elements
■ Inherited: yes

This is a shorthand property for setting 'font-style', 'font-variant', 'font-weight', 'font-size', 'line-height', and 'font-family'.

Font properties are first reset to their initial value. Those properties that are given explicit values in the 'font' shorthand property are set to those values. The 'font' property is set in the following order.

1. 'font-style', 'font-variant', and 'font-weight' values may be omitted or may appear in any order.
2. The 'font-size' value cannot be omitted.
3. The 'line-height' value is optional. font-size and line-height values are separated by '/': for example, `9.5pt`/`13`pt.
4. The 'font-family' value cannot be omitted. Multiple font families are separated by commas.

```
.CoverPage h1 {   /* document title*/
    font: bold 30pt Meiryo, sans-serif;
}
```

Additional Fonts : @font-face rule 🖺

Allows additional fonts without altering your AH Formatter settings and without installing the font in your operating system. The following descriptors are allowed:

- 'font-family' : Name to use in CSS font family name matching. Overrides family name from font data.
- 'src' : Location of font resource. May be an alias of an existing local font.
- 'font-style' : Optional font style characteristic to use when matching fonts. May be 'italic' or 'normal'. The default value is 'normal'.
- 'font-weight' : Optional font weight characteristic to use when matching fonts. Use the same values as the 'font-weight' property except that the 'bolder' and 'lighter' relative keywords are not allowed. The default value is 'normal'.

```
@font-face {
    font-family: font-face-example;
    src: url(UglyQua.ttf);
}

p { font-family: font-face-example; }
```

The Quick Brown Fox

Vertical Alignment : 'vertical-align'

■ Initial value: 'baseline'   ■ Applies to: inline-level and table cell elements
■ Inherited: no

Vertical alignment, such as for superscripts and subscripts, can be specified.
- 'normal' : standard alignment
- 'baseline' : Align to the baseline of the parent element.
- 'sub' : subscript.
- 'super' : superscript.
- 'top' : Align to the top edge.
- 'text-top' : Align to the top edge of the text.
- 'middle' : Align to center.
- 'bottom' : Align to bottom edge.
- 'text-bottom' : Align to the bottom edge of the text.
- <percentage> : Sets the value as a percentage of the line height. 0% is the same as 'baseline'.
- <length> : Raise or lower the box by this distance. 0 is the same as 'baseline'.

A subset of the 'vertical-align' values also apply to table cells, but with different meanings. See Vertical Alignment in Table Cells (page 80).

Underline, Overline, and Line-through Decorations

Text decoration lines : 'text-decoration-line' 🗐

■ Initial value: 'none'   ■ Applies to: all elements   ■ Inherited: no

Specifies underlines, overlines, and lines-through to the text. When setting more than one value at the same time, specify them in any order separated by spaces.
- 'none' : Adds no text decoration.
- 'underline' : Each line is underlined.
- 'overline' : Each line has a line above it.
- 'line-through' : Each line of text has a line through the middle.

```
.Chapter h2 {
    text-decoration-line: underline overline;
}
```

Line type : 'text-decoration-style' ▤

■ Initial value: 'solid' ■ Applies to: all elements ■ Inherited: no

Specifies different types of underlines, overlines, and line-through decorations. The same values can be used as for specifying the style of a single border of a box. See Border Style : 'border-style' (page 144) for details.

```
span.solid {
  text-decoration-style: solid;     /* make the line style solid */
}
span.wave {
  text-decoration-style: wave;      /* make the line style wavy */
}

solid : <span class="solid">solid line</span>
wave : <span class="wave">wavy line</span>
```

Line color : 'text-decoration-color' ▤

■ Initial value: current color ■ Applies to: all elements ■ Inherited: no

Specifies the color of underlines, overlines, and line-through text decorations. See 17. COLOR (page 135) for details.

```
span {
  text-decoration-color: cmyk(0,1,1,0);   /* make line color red */
}
```

Text decoration shorthand : 'text-decoration' ▤

■ Initial value: 'none' ■ Applies to: all elements ■ Inherited: no

Specifies the type, color, and style of underline, overline, and line-through text decorations. 'text-decoration' is a shorthand for setting 'text-decoration-line', 'text-decoration-color', and 'text-decoration-style' in one declaration. A 'text-decoration' property that sets only the 'text-decoration-line' component is backwards-compatible with CSS 2.

```
span {
  text-decoration: underline dotted cmyk(0,1,1,0);   /* Red */
}
```

Line width : '-ah-text-line-width' ◪

■ Initial value: 'auto' ■ Applies to: all elements ■ Inherited: no

Specifies the line width for underlines, overlines, and line-throughs. See Border Thickness : 'border-width' (page 143) for details.

JAPANESE TEXT COMPOSITION

Japanese text has its own conventions and rules. *Requirements for Japanese Text Layout* (JLReq) from the W3C is a good English-language resource for learning more.

A feature of Japanese typography is that every character occupies a 1em square. Most characters used in Japanese text fill the 1em square. However, some punctuation characters typically make a mark in only one half or the other of the width of the 1em square: for example, " 〔", "〕 ", " 『", "』 ", "。 ", and "、 ". CSS defines some properties that control how to handle these characters at the start or end of lines or when multiple of these characters occur together. AH Formatter provides additional properties for finer control of these characters.

Two other features of Japanese layout are Tatechuyoko (text set horizontally within vertical text) and Ruby (small text annotations added to base characters).

Fixed Trimming of Start and End Line Punctuation – Paragraph Start Line Indent

The convention for Japanese text composition is that a fullwidth punctuation character is trimmed if it appears at the start/end of a line or is adjacent to another fullwidth punctuation character and the start indent of a new paragraph is 1em.

- Line start punctuation : Trims fullwidth punctuation glyphs.
- Line end punctuation : Trims the blank half of fullwidth punctuation glyphs.
- First line indent : 1em indent on the first line of a new paragraph.

```
body {   /* setup for Japanese document composition */
  punctuation-trim: start end adjacent;
  -ah-text-justify-trim: punctuation;
  -ah-text-autospace: ideograph-numeric ideograph-alpha;
  -ah-text-autospace-width: 25%;
  hanging-punctuation: none;
}

p {     /* paragraph */
  text-align: justify;   /* line end align */
  text-indent: 1em;  /* set 1em for first line indent in a paragraph*/
```

```
    margin: 0;        /* no margin between paragraphs */
}
```

夏目漱石（なつめ そうせき、慶応三年一月五日（一八六七年二月九日）—大正五年（一九一六年）一二月九日）は、日本の小説家、評論家、英文学者。本名、金之助。『吾輩は猫である』『こゝろ』などの作品で広く知られる。森鷗外と並ぶ明治・大正時代の文豪である。江戸の牛込馬場下横町（現在の東京都新宿区喜久井町）出身。俳号は愚陀仏。

大学時代に正岡子規と出会い、俳句を学ぶ。…（中略）…当初は余裕派と呼ばれた。「修善寺の大患」後は、『行人』『こゝろ』『硝子戸の中』などを執筆。『則天去私』（そくてんきょし）の境地に達したといわれる。晩年は胃潰瘍に悩まされ、『明暗』が絶筆となった。

フリー百科事典『ウィキペディア』より引用∨

Fullwidth Punctuation Trimming : 'punctuation-trim'

▪ Initial value: 'none' ▪ Applies to: block elements ▪ Inherited: yes

Specifies how to treat fullwidth punctuation at the start or end of a line.

- 'none' : Punctuation characters are not trimmed.
- 'start' : Punctuation characters (open parenthesis, etc.) at the start of a line are trimmed.
- 'start-except-first' : Same as 'start' except for the first line of a paragraph or the line right after a forced line break.
- 'end' : When `text-align: right` and `text-align: justify` (or `text-align-last: justify`) are specified, fullwidth punctuation glyphs (closing parenthesis, etc.) at the end of a sentence are forcibly treated as halfwidth.
- 'allow-end' : When `text-align: right` and `text-align: justify` (or `text-align-last: justify`) are specified, fullwidth punctuation glyphs (closing brackets, etc.) at the end of a sentence are treated as fullwidth if the text fits into one line; the characters are treated as if text does not fit into one line.
- 'end-except-fullstop' : Behaves the same as the 'end' value except for the following two characters.
  - U+3002 = "。 "
  - U+FF0E = "． "

- 'adjacent' : In Japanese, the space between a fullwidth punctuation glyph and a fullwidth character is trimmed. Spaces to be treated are the following. Fullwidth punctuations glyphs and fullwidth closing parentheses are treated the same way.
  - Between fullwidth close parenthesis and fullwidth open parenthesis.
  - Between fullwidth close parenthesis and fullwidth close parenthesis.
  - Between fullwidth close parenthesis and fullwidth middle dots.
  - Between fullwidth close parenthesis and fullwidth space.
  - Between fullwidth close parenthesis and fullwidth non punctuation characters.
  - Between fullwidth open parenthesis and fullwidth open parenthesis.
  - Between fullwidth middle dots and fullwidth open parenthesis.
  - Between fullwidth space and fullwidth open parenthesis.
  - Between fullwidth non punctuation character and fullwidth open parenthesis.
- 'all' : Same as 'all' except that the characters in the string are treated as halfwidth.
- <string> : Trim all parentheses, middle dots, and fullwidth punctuation and treat them as halfwidth.
- 'auto' : Depends on the system setting.

When successive punctuation (punctuation marks and brackets) glyphs come at the start or end of a line, the fullwidth characters are trimmed, improving the appearance of the text.

```
/* fullwidth punctuation character is trimmed at the start or end of
   a line, or adjacent to another fullwidth punctuation character */
punctuation-trim: start end adjacent;
```

「《約物〔やくもの〕》、つまり『括弧』・『句読点』の類 (たぐい) です。」

The following example shows when punctuation trim is deactivated. (Specify `punctuation-trim: none;`)

「 《約物〔やくもの〕》 、 つまり『括弧』 ・ 『句読点』 の類 (たぐい) です 。 」

Additional Compression : '-ah-text-justify-trim'

■ Initial value: 'none'   ■ Applies to: all elements   ■ Inherited: yes

Specifies different ways of compressing Japanese text. It specifies how to trim spaces so that the text fits within a line.
- 'none' : Do not trim Japanese text.

- 'punctuation' : Trim fullwidth parentheses, middle dots, and punctuation glyphs.
- 'punctuation-except-fullstop' : Behaves the same as the 'punctuation' value except for the following two characters.
  - U+3002 = " 。 "
  - U+FF0E = " ． "
- punctuation-except-middledot: Behaves the same as the 'punctuation' value except for the following middle dots.
  - U+30FB = " ・ "
  - U+FF1A = " ： "
  - U+FF1B = " ； "
- 'kana' : Trim kana (Hiragana and Katakana) glyphs just a little bit.
- 'ideograph' : Trim spaces between kana or kanji.
- 'inter-word' : Trim spaces between Western words.
- 'auto' : Depends on the system setting.

```
/* punctuation trimming allowed for adjusting lines */
-ah-text-justify-trim: punctuation;
```

Automatically reverts the punctuation glyphs that were trimmed (before fullwidth opening parentheses and after fullwidth closing parentheses and punctuation marks), to fullwidth so the text fills the line, as described in the previous section.

Adding Space : '-ah-text-autospace'

█ Initial value: 'none'   █ Applies to: block elements   █ Inherited: yes

Specifies whether or not to add space between ideographic glyphs in Japanese.
- 'none' : No extra space is added.
- 'ideograph-numeric' : Adds a space between Kana/Kanji and Western letters.
- 'ideograph-alpha' : Adds a space between Kana/Kanji and Western alphabetic characters.
- 'ideograph-parenthesis' : Adds a space between Kana/Kanji and Western brackets. However, no extra space is added between Kana/Kanji and Western closing brackets or between Western opening brackets and Kana/Kanji.
- 'ideograph-punctuation' : Adds a space between Kana/Kanji and Western punctuation. Adds a space between periods and Kana/Kanji, but does not add space between Kana/Kanji and periods. The same goes for commas.
- 'auto' : Depending on the system setting, it is regarded as none or `ideograph-numeric ideograph-alpha`.

Therefore, if a mixture of Western texts and Arabic numerals are included in Japanese sentences, a little bit of space is added between them to make it easier to read.

```
/* Add space between kanji, kana, and numbers and between kanji,
   kana, and Western texts */
-ah-text-autospace: ideograph-numeric ideograph-alpha;
```

For comparison, the following example shows that setting `-ah-text-auto-space: none;`, spacing between Japanese letters and alphabets will be deactivated.

「日本語にも global にも 100%を目指す AH Formatter です」

「日本語にもglobalにも100%を目指すAH Formatterです」

Amount of Space Between Japanese and Western Text : '-ah-text-autospace-width'

■ Initial value: 25%   ■ Applies to: block elements   ■ Inherited: yes
Specifies the amount of space between Japanese and Western text in Japanese.

```
/* amount of space between Japanese and Western text */
-ah-text-autospace-width: 25%;   /* Initial value */
```

Hanging Punctuation : 'hanging-punctuation'

■ Initial value: 'none'   ■ Applies to: block elements   ■ Inherited: yes
Specifies whether punctuation marks at the start or at the end of a line hang into the margins.

- 'none' : Does not hang punctuation marks at the start or at the end of a line.
- 'start' : Hangs punctuation marks at the start of a line. If the character to be hung appears at the start of a line, it is forced to hang.
- 'first' : Behaves as the 'start' value but only for the first line of a paragraph.
- 'force-end' : Hangs punctuation marks at the end of the line. If `text-align: right` or `text-align: justify` (or `text-align-last: justify`) is specified and the character that can be hung appears at the end of a line, it is forced to hang. If anything else is specified for text-align, it is naturally hung.
- 'allow-end' : Hangs punctuation marks at the end of a line. If `text-align: right` or `text-align: justify` (or `text-align-last: justify`) is specified and the character to be hung appears at the end of the line; it is not hung if the text fits into one line. It is hung if the text does not fit into one line. If anything else is specified for 'text-align', it is naturally hung.
- 'last' : Behaves as the 'force-end' value but only for the last line of a paragraph.

Punctuation marks allowed to hang are as follows:
- 'force-end', 'allow-end'

Japanese or Simplified Chinese:
- U+3001 = "、 "
- U+3002 = "。 "
- U+FF0C = "， "
- U+FF0E = "． "

Traditional Chinese:
- U+FE50
- U+FE51
- U+FE52
- U+FF64

Other languages:
- Same as the 'last' value

- 'last'

  quotation marks, closing parentheses, periods, commas, and hyphens
- 'start', 'first'

  quotation marks, closing parentheses, and bullet

```
/* specifies whether to hang punctuation marks at the start or
   at the end of a line. */
hanging-punctuation: none;   /* Initial value */
```

Trimming Line Start Punctuation – Fullwidth/Halfwidth Line End Punctuation – First Line Indent of a New Paragraph

Allows trimming of line-start punctuation, fullwidth and halfwidth line-end punctuation, and indents the first line of a new paragraph 1em.

- Line start punctuation : Trim fullwidth punctuation glyphs.
- Line end punctuation : Trim fullwidth and halfwidth punctuation marks.
- First line indent : Indent 1em at the first line of a new paragraph.

```
body {
    /* setup for Japanese document composition */
    punctuation-trim: start allow-end adjacent;
    -ah-text-justify-trim: punctuation;
    -ah-text-autospace: ideograph-numeric ideograph-alpha;
    -ah-text-autospace-width: 25%;
    hanging-punctuation: none;
}

p {      /* paragraph */
    text-align: justify;   /* line end align */
    text-indent: 1em; /* set 1em for first line indent in a paragraph*/
    margin: 0;          /* no margin between paragraphs */
}
```

夏目漱石（なつめ そうせき、慶応三年一月五日（一八六七年二月九日）－大正五年（一九一六年）一二月九日）は、日本の小説家、評論家、英文学者。本名、金之助。『吾輩は猫である』『こゝろ』などの作品で広く知られる、森鷗外と並ぶ明治・大正時代の文豪である。

江戸の牛込馬場下横町（現在の東京都新宿区喜久井町）出身。俳号は愚陀仏。

大学時代に正岡子規と出会い、俳句を学ぶ。

…（中略）…当初は余裕派と呼ばれた。

「修善寺の大患」後は、『行人』『こゝろ』『硝子戸の中』などを執筆。「則天去私」（そくてんきょし）の境地に達したといわれる。晩年は胃潰瘍に悩まされ、『明暗』が絶筆となった。

フリー百科事典『ウィキペディア』より

引用

Trimming Line Start Punctuation – Fullwidth Line End Punctuation – First Line Indent of a New Paragraph.

Trim line start punctuation – Fullwidth line end punctuation only – Indent the start of a line 1em.

- Line start punctuation : Trim fullwidth punctuation glyphs.
- Line end punctuation : Trim fullwidth punctuation glyphs, others are assumed trimmed.
- First line indent : Indent 1em at the first line of a new paragraph.

```
body {
    /* setup for Japanese document composition */
    punctuation-trim: start end-except-fullstop adjacent;
    -ah-text-justify-trim: punctuation;
    -ah-text-autospace: ideograph-numeric ideograph-alpha;
    -ah-text-autospace-width: 25%;
    hanging-punctuation: none;
}

p {      /* paragraph */
    text-align: justify;   /* line end align */
    text-indent: 1em; /* set 1em for first line indent in a paragraph*/
    margin: 0;          /* no margin between paragraphs */
}
```

夏目漱石（なつめ そうせき、慶応三年一月五日（一八六七年二月九日）―大正五年（一九一六年）二月九日）は、日本の小説家、評論家、英文学者。本名、金之助。『吾輩は猫である』『こゝろ』などの作品で広く知られる、森鷗外と並ぶ明治・大正時代の文豪である。

江戸の牛込馬場下横町（現在の東京都新宿区喜久井町）出身。俳号は愚陀仏。

大学時代に正岡子規と出会い、俳句を学ぶ。…（中略）…当初は余裕派と呼ばれた。

「修善寺の大患」後は、『行人』『こゝろ』『硝子戸の中』などを執筆。「則天去私」（そくてんきょし）の境地に達したといわれる。晩年は胃潰瘍に悩まされ、『明暗』が絶筆となった。

フリー百科事典『ウィキペディア』より引用

Trimming Line Start and Line End Punctuation – First Line Indent of a New Paragraph

Trim line start punctuation – Trim line end punctuation – Indent opening parentheses at the beginning of the paragraph by 0.5 em.

- Line start punctuation : Trim fullwidth punctuation glyphs.
- Line end punctuation : Trim the blank half of fullwidth punctuation glyphs.
- First line indent : Indent 1em at the first line of a new paragraph and indent punctuation 0.5em.

```
body {
    /* setup for Japanese document composition */
    punctuation-trim: start end adjacent;
    -ah-text-justify-trim: punctuation;
    -ah-text-autospace: ideograph-numeric ideograph-alpha;
    -ah-text-autospace-width: 25%;
    hanging-punctuation: first;
}
p {      /* paragraph */
    text-align: justify;   /* line end align */
    text-indent: 1em;  /* set 1em for first line indent in a paragraph*/
    margin: 0;           /* no margin between paragraphs */
}
```

夏目漱石（なつめ そうせき、慶応三年一月
五日（一八六七年二月九日）―大正五年（一九一
六年）一二月九日）は、日本の小説家、評論
家、英文学者。本名、金之助。『吾輩は猫で
ある』『こゝろ』などの作品で広く知られる、
森鷗外と並ぶ明治・大正時代の文豪である。
江戸の牛込馬場下横町（現在の東京都新宿区
喜久井町）出身。俳号は愚陀仏。
大学時代に正岡子規と出会い、俳句を学
ぶ。…（中略）…当初は余裕派と呼ばれた。
『修善寺の大患』後は、『行人』『こゝろ』
『硝子戸の中』などを執筆。「則天去私」
（そくてんきょし）の境地に達したといわれる。
晩年は胃潰瘍に悩まされ、『明暗』が絶筆と
なった。
フリー百科事典『ウィキペディア』より
引用

Horizontal-in-Vertical Composition (Tatechuyoko)

Specifies words in the horizontal orientation within a vertical writing mode. (Numbers, etc. in a vertical line are written in a horizontal orientation).

```css
/* horizontal-in-vertical composition */
span.TateChuYoko {
  /* create a small block in the middle of a row */
  display: inline-block;
  /* set this small block in horizontal orientation*/
  writing-mode: lr-tb;
  /* align text to center */
  text-align: center;
  /* no text indent (erase text-indents from the paragraph) */
  text-indent: 0;
  /* set line gap not to overlap above and below
     TATECHUYOKO (horizontal-in-vertical composition) */
  line-height: 1;
}
```

```html
<div class="VerticalTextBlock">
  …
  <p>縦書きの中に「<span class="TateChuYoko">'08</span>年
  <span class="TateChuYoko">12</span>月
  <span class="TateChuYoko">8</span>日」
  のように部分的に数字などを横書きにすることを「縦中横」といいます。 </p>
</div>
```

縦書きの中に「'08年12月8日」のように部分的に数字などを横書きにすることを「縦中横」といいます。

Ruby and Emphasis Marks

In XHTML, when using the `<ruby>` element, emphasis marks can be applied to the ruby characters (Furigana). Specify the base character (characters that are to be applied with ruby) with the `<rb>` element and specify the ruby characters (the contents of the ruby) with the `<rt>` element.

The following CSS shows a sample application of ruby.

```
/* Ruby (from 'html.css') */
ruby    { display: ruby }
rb      { display: ruby-base }
rt      { display: ruby-text }
rp      { display: none }
```

```
<p><ruby><rb>吾輩</rb><rp>（</rp><rt>わがはい</rt><rp>）</rp></ruby>は猫である。
</p>
<p>名前はまだ無い。どこで生れたかとんと<ruby><rb>見当</rb><rp>（</rp><rt>けんとう</rt><rp>）</rp></ruby>がつかぬ。</p>
```

Horizontal Writing Mode

吾輩は猫である。

名前はまだ無い。どこで生れたかとんと見当がつかぬ。

Vertical Writing Mode

吾輩は猫である。名前はまだ無い。どこで生れたかとんと見当がつかぬ。

AH Formatter can add emphasis marks to CJK text as well as to text in the Latn, Cyrl, Grek, and Zyyy scripts.

```
/* emphasis mark */
span.kenten {
  -ah-text-emphasis-style: filled;
  -ah-text-emphasis-offset: 0.25;
  -ah-text-emphasis-font-size: 0.25;
}
```

```
<p>ここを<span class="kenten">圏点で強調</span>します．</p>
```

ここを圏点で強調します．

CROSS-REFERENCES

The hard and brittle way to create cross-references is to write hard-coded text for cross-references to the title or the number of the chapter, section, figure or other component to which you are referring. You could also write hard-coded page numbers.

The simpler and more resilient way is to use the 'target-text()' and 'target-counter()' functions refer to another element by its ID and to generate the cross-reference. They can, respectively, generate either the text content of another element or a representation of the value of a counter that is associated with that element. In paged media, 'target-counter()' can also generate the page number of that element.

Text Contents Reference : 'target-text()' function 🔲

Use the 'target-text()' function to display a textual reference as the source reference.
Cross-references using the 'target-text()' function operate as follows:

1. Specify a character string to be inserted into the source reference in the CSS file.
2. A variable counter specified in 'target-text()' function can be inserted using the 'content' property and the 'target-text()' function.
3. Insert an `<a>` element as an anchor inside the sentence source reference and specify the cross-reference class name for that class. In addition, specify the source reference ID value in the `href` attribute.
4. The character string in the anchor element replaces the reference string.

```
.TitleRef {
  content: target-text(attr(href url), before) ", "
           target-text(attr(href url), content);
}

<section class="Chapter">
<h2 id="CRef">Cross-References</h2>

<p>Example : "<a class="TitleRef" href="#CRef">This chapter</a>"</p>
<p>The referenced title replaces 'This chapter'.</p>
```

Counter Reference : 'target-counter()' function

Use the 'target-counter()' function to automatically add a reference to chapter and/or page number. See 16. COUNTERS (page 125) for details.
    Cross-references using the 'target-counter()' function operate as follows:
1. In the CSS style sheet, specify a string that is to be inserted as the content of the '::before' or '::after' pseudo-element.
2. With 'target-counter()', the variable specified in the 'target-counter()' function can be inserted using the 'content' property. To insert a literal string, put double or single quotation marks around the string. Also, separate it from the 'target-counter()' function with spaces.
3. Insert an <a> element as an anchor inside the sentence source reference and specify the cross-reference class name for that class. In addition, specify the source reference ID value in the href attribute.

```
.ChapterRef::before {
  content: target-counter(attr(href url), ChapterNo) ". "
           target-text(attr(href url), content);
  font-variant: all-small-caps;
}

.PageRef::after {
  content: "(page " target-counter(attr(href url), page) ")";
  font-variant: oldstyle-nums proportional-nums;
}
```

```
<section class="Chapter">
<h2 id="Counters">Counters</h2>

See <a class="ChapterRef PageRef" href="#Counters">Counter</a>
for details.
```

See 16. COUNTERS (page 125) for details.

Creating a Table of Contents

A table of contents can be created with the 'target-counter()' function which can refer to chapter and page numbers.

```
/* add chapter number to the table of contents */
.TOC a::before {
```

```
  content: "Chapter " target-counter(attr(href url), ChapterNo)
           ". ";
}
/* add page number to the table of contents */
.TOC a::after {
  content: leader(space) " " target-counter(attr(href url), page);
}

<div class="TOC">
  <ul>
    <li class="TocLevel1">
      <a href="#WebvsPrint">Screen and Paged Media</a>
    </li>
    <li class="TocLevel1">
      <a href="#BoxModel">Box Layout</a>
    </li>
    <li class="TocLevel1">
      <a href="#ObjectDecorate">Background Decoration</a>
    </li>
    ...
  </ul>
</div>
```

An example Table of Contents	
Chapter 1. Screen & Paged Media	5
Chapter 2. Box Layout	11
Chapter 3. Page Layout	21
Chapter 4. Headers & Footers	35
Chapter 5. Multiple Columns	47
Chapter 6. Keeps & Breaks	51
Chapter 7. Paragraph Setting	55

IMAGE POSITIONING

CSS supports positioning an image inline with surrounding text, as a separate block, or floated to the right, left, or center. AH Formatter implements the ability to float an image to the top or bottom of either the page or the containing block, as well as the ability to size a float to span a specified width within a multi-column layout.

Inline Image

Use the inline `<img>` and `<object>` image elements to place an inline image in a sentence.

```
<p style="text-indent: 0">Antenna House <img src="images/logo-
antenna.svg" alt="AH logo" style="height: 9pt;" /> Formatter is the
most powerful XSL-FO software and CSS document formatting software on
the market. To meet your needs, we have expanded AH Formatter to…
```

Inline Image

Antenna House █ Formatter is the most powerful XSL-FO software and CSS document formatting software on the market. To meet your needs, we have expanded AH Formatter to support more than 70 languages.

AH Formatter ▣ features support for PDF/UA and improved CGM rendering. It also includes support for MathML V3.0, layered PDFs, enhanced support for embedding multimedia and numerous extensions.

Block image

Use `display: block;` to make an image display as a block rather than inline.

```
<p>Antenna House <img src="images/logo-antenna.svg" alt="AH logo"
style="display: block; height: 9pt;" /> Formatter is the most
powerful XSL-FO software and CSS document formatting software on the
market. To meet your needs, we have expanded AH Formatter to…
```

An inline image set with display: block;

Antenna House

Formatter is the most powerful XSL-FO software and CSS document formatting software on the market. To meet your needs, we have expanded AH Formatter to support more than 70 languages.
AH Formatter

features support for PDF/UA and improved CGM rendering. It also includes support for MathML V3.0, layered PDFs, enhanced support for embedding multimedia and numerous extensions.

Positioning as a Float : 'float'

■ Initial value: 'none'   ■ Applies to: all elements   ■ Inherited: no

Use the 'float' property to float the image and set it to float either to the left, right, or not at all. AH Formatter provides extensions for arranging the floated element at an arbitrary place on the page.

Side float : `float: left` / `float: right`
Any adjacent element wraps around the other side of the element that has the 'float' property.

```
<p style="text-indent: 0">
<img src="images/logo-antenna.svg" style="float: left; height: 3em;
margin-left: 9pt;" />Antenna House Formatter is the most powerful XSL-
FO software and CSS document formatting software on the market. To
meet your needs, we have expanded AH Formatter to…
```

left-aligned image: `float: left;`

Antenna House Formatter is the most powerful XSL-FO software and CSS document formatting software on the market. To meet your needs, we have expanded AH Formatter to support more than 70 languages. AH Formatter features support for PDF/UA and improved CGM rendering. It also includes support for MathML V3.0, layered PDFs, enhanced support for embedding multimedia and numerous extensions.

```
<p style="text-indent: 0">
<img src="images/logo-antenna.svg" style="float: right; height:3em;
margin-right: 9pt;" />Antenna House Formatter is the most powerful
XSL-FO software and CSS document formatting software on the market.
To meet your needs, we have expanded AH Formatter to…
```

> This is at the top of the page. Specified by `float: top page`.

> This is the second top float for the page. Specified by `float: top page`.

Right-aligned image: `float: right;`

Antenna House Formatter is the most powerful XSL-FO software and CSS document formatting software on the market. To meet your needs, we have expanded AH Formatter to support more than 70 languages.
AH Formatter features support for PDF/UA and improved CGM rendering. It also includes support for MathML V3.0, layered PDFs, enhanced support for embedding multimedia and numerous extensions.

Text as well as images can be floated[1].

left-aligned text: `float: left;`

Antenna House   Formatter is the most powerful XSL-FO software and CSS document formatting software on the market.

Right-aligned text: `float: right;`

Formatter is the most powerful XSL-FO software and CSS document formatting software on the market. Antenna House

Page float : `float: top page` / `float: bottom page`
In the existing HTML and CSS layouts, it is common to use `float: left;` and `float: right;` to align images and characters to the left and right of the body text. Page floats extend this to the vertical direction.

    `float: top page;` positions a block at the top of the page. `float: bottom page;` places a block at the end of the page.

    Two page float examples are shown at both the top and bottom of this page.[2]

> This is the second bottom float for the page. Specified by `float: bottom page`.

> This is the end of the page. Specified by `float: bottom page`.

---

1 It is not common to indent right after a display heading, but indentation is done here for comparison with the right-aligned float.
2 Or on the next page if there is not enough space available on this page.

```
<div style="float: top page; border: ridge maroon; padding: 3pt;
margin-bottom: 1em;">
<p>This is the top page. Specified by <b>float: top page</b>. </p>
</div>
<div style="float: bottom page; border: ridge green; padding: 3pt;
margin-top: 1em;">
<p>This is the bottom page. Specified by <b>float: bottom page</b>.
</p></div>
```

Column float : `float: top` / `float: bottom` 🔳

`float: top;` positions the block at the top of the column. `float: bottom;`
positions the block at the bottom of the column.

```
<p>Whereas recognition of the inherent dignity and…</p>
<div style="float: bottom; border: ridge lime; padding: 3pt;">
<p>This is the bottom of the column. Specified by <b>float:
bottom</b>.</p></div>
<p>Whereas disregard and contempt for human rights have…</p>
<div style="float: top; border: ridge orange; padding: 3pt;">
<p>This is the top of the column. Specified by <b>float: top</b>.
</p></div>
<p>Whereas it is essential, if man is not to be compelled…</p>
```

> Whereas recognition of the inherent di-
> gnity and of the equal and inalienable
> rights of all members of the human fa-
> mily is the foundation of freedom, ju-
> stice and peace in the world,
> Whereas disregard and contempt for
> human rights have resulted in barba-
> rous acts which have outraged the con-
> science of mankind, and the advent of
> a world in which human beings shall
>
> > This is the bottom of the column.
> > Specified by float: bottom.
>
> This is the top of the column.
> Specified by float: top.
>
> enjoy freedom of speech and belief and
> freedom from fear and want has been
> proclaimed as the highest aspiration of
> the common people,
> Whereas it is essential, if man is not to
> be compelled to have recourse, as a last
> resort, to rebellion against tyranny and
> oppression, that human rights should
> be protected by the rule of law,

Inside, outside and alternate float : `float: inside` / `float: outside` / `float: alternate` 🔳

`float: inside;` positions the block on the left side on a right-hand page or on
the right side on a left-hand page.

Whereas recognition of the inherent dignity and of the equal and inalienable rights of all members of the human family is the foundation of freedom, justice and peace in the world, `float: inside` Whereas disregard and contempt for human rights have resulted in barbarous acts which have outraged the conscience of mankind, and the advent of a world in which human beings shall enjoy freedom of speech and belief and freedom from fear and want has been proclaimed as the highest aspiration of the common people, `float: inside` Whereas it is essential, if man is not to be compelled to have recourse, as a last resort, to rebellion against tyranny and oppression, that human rights should be protected by the rule of law,

`float: outside`; positions the block at the right side on a right-hand page or on the left side on a left-hand page.

Whereas recognition of the inherent dignity and of the equal and inalienable rights of all members of the human family is the foundation of freedom, justice and peace in the world, Whereas disregard and contempt for human `float: outside` rights have resulted in barbarous acts which have outraged the conscience of mankind, and the advent of a world in which human beings shall enjoy freedom of speech and belief and freedom from fear and want has been proclaimed as the highest aspiration of the common people, Whereas it is essential, if man is not to be compelled to have recourse, as a last resort, `float: outside` to rebellion against tyranny and oppression, that human rights should be protected by the rule of law,

`float: center`; positions the block at the center of the column.

Whereas recognition of the inherent dignity and of the equal and inalienable rights of all members of the human family is the foundation of freedom, justice and peace in the world, `float: center` Whereas disregard and contempt for human rights have resulted in barbarous acts which have outraged the conscience of mankind, and the advent of a world in which human beings shall enjoy freedom of speech and belief and freedom from fear and want has been proclaimed as the highest aspiration of the common people, `float: center` Whereas it is essential, if man is not to be compelled to have recourse, as a last resort, to rebellion against tyranny and oppression, that human rights should be protected by the rule of law, `float: start;` positions the block on the start side. This is the same as 'left' in horizontal left-to-right writing mode.

Whereas recognition of the inherent di-gnity and of the equal and inalienable rights of all members of the human fa-mily is the foundation of freedom, ju-stice and peace in the world, `float: start` Whereas disregard and contempt for human rights have resulted in barbarous acts which have outraged the conscience of mankind, and the advent of a world in which human beings shall enjoy freedom of speech and belief and free-dom from fear and want has been pro-claimed as the highest aspiration of the common people, `float: start` Whereas it is essential, if man is not to be compel-led to have recourse, as a last resort, to rebellion against tyranny and oppres-sion, that human rights should be pro-tected by the rule of law,

It is the same as 'right' in horizontal right-to-left writing mode.

ואיל והכרה בכבוד הטבעי אשר `float: start` לכל בני משפהת האדם ובזכויותיהם השוות והבלתי נפקעות הוא יסוד החופש, הצדק והשלום בעולם`float: start`. הואיל והזלזול בזכויות האדם וביזיון הבשילו מעשים `float: start` פראיים שפגעו קשה במצפונה של האנושות; ובנין עולם, שבו ייהנו כל יצורי אנוש מחירות הדיבור והאמונה ומן החירות מפחד וממחסור, הוכרז כראש שאיפותיו של כל אדם. הואיל והכרח חיוני הוא `float: start` שזכויות האדם תהיינה מוגנות בכוח שלטונו של החוק, שלא יהא האדם אנוס, כמפלט אחרון, להשליך את יהבו על מרידה בעריצות ובדיכזי. `float: start` `float: start`

`float: end;` positions the block on the end side. This is the same as 'right' in horizontal left-to-right writing mode.

Whereas recognition of the inherent dignity and of the equal and inalienable rights of all members of the human family is the foundation of freedom, justice and peace in the world, Whereas disregard and contempt for human `float: end` rights have resulted in barbarous acts which have outraged the conscience of mankind, and the advent of a world in which human beings shall enjoy freedom of speech and belief and free-dom from fear and want has been pro-claimed as the highest aspiration of the common people, Whereas it is essential, if man is not to be compel-led to have recourse, as a last resort, to rebellion against tyranny and oppres-sion, that human rights should be pro-tected by the rule of law, `float: end`

It is the same as 'left' in horizontal right-to-left writing mode.

ואיל והכרה בכבוד הטבעי אשר לכל בני משפהת האדם ובזכויותיהם השוות והבלתי נפקעות הוא יסוד החופש, הצדק והשלום בעולם.
הואיל והזלזול בזכויות האדם `float: end` וביזוין הבשילו מעשים פראיים שפגעו קשה במצפונה של האנושות; ובנין עולם, שבו ייהנו כל יצורי אנוש מחירות הדיבור

והאמונה ומן החירות מפחד וממחסור, הוכרז כראש שאיפותיו של כל אדם.
הואיל והכרח חיוני הוא `float: end` שזכויות האדם תהיינה מוגנות בכוח שלטונו של החוק, שלא יהא האדם אנוס, כמפלט אחרון, להשליך את יהבו על מרידה בעריצות ובדיכזי.

`float: alternate;` positions a block in the first column as if 'end' is specified, a block in the last column as if 'start' is specified, and a block in any other column as if 'center' is specified.

Whereas recognition of the inherent dignity and of the equal and inalienable rights of all members of the human family is the foundation of freedom, justice and peace in the world,

Whereas disregard `float: alternate` and contempt for hu-man rights have resulted in barbarous acts which have outraged the conscience of mankind, and the advent of a world in which human beings shall

enjoy freedom of speech and belief and freedom from fear and want has been proclaimed as the highest aspiration of the common people,

`float: alternate` Whereas it is essential, if man is not to be compelled to have recourse, as a last resort, to rebellion against tyranny and oppression, that human rights should be protected by the rule of law,

14

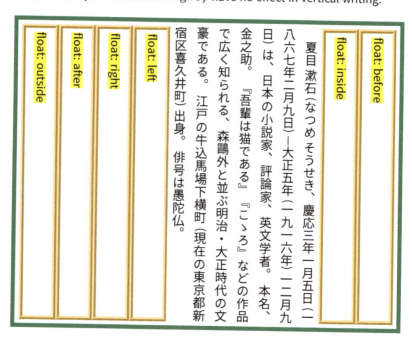

夏目漱石（なつめ そうせき、慶応三年一月五日（一八六七年二月九日）—大正五年（一九一六年）二月九日）は、日本の小説家、評論家、英文学者。本名、金之助。『吾輩は猫である』『こゝろ』などの作品で広く知られる、森鴎外と並ぶ明治・大正時代の文豪である。江戸の牛込馬場下横町（現在の東京都新宿区喜久井町）出身。俳号は愚陀仏。

[float: top]

大学時代に正岡子規と出会い、俳句を学ぶ。…（中略）…当初は余裕派と呼ばれた。

「修善寺の大患」後は、『行人』『こゝろ』『硝子戸の中』『則天去私』（そくてんきょし）などを執筆。「修善寺の大患」後は、『行人』『こゝろ』『硝子戸の中』『則天去私』（そくてんきょし）の境地に達したといわれる。晩年は胃潰瘍に悩まされ、『明暗』が絶筆となった。

[float: center]

[float: bottom]

フリー百科事典『ウィキペディア』より引用〉

`float: left`; and `float: right`; have no effect in vertical writing.

夏目漱石（なつめ そうせき、慶応三年一月五日（一八六七年二月九日）—大正五年（一九一六年）二月九日）は、日本の小説家、評論家、英文学者。本名、金之助。『吾輩は猫である』『こゝろ』などの作品で広く知られる、森鴎外と並ぶ明治・大正時代の文豪である。江戸の牛込馬場下横町（現在の東京都新宿区喜久井町）出身。俳号は愚陀仏。

[float: before] [float: inside] [float: left] [float: right] [float: after] [float: outside]

14

Multi-column float : float: multicol ⧉

`float: multicol;` allows the float to span multiple columns plus the gaps between the columns. The 'gr' length unit denotes the width of either a column or column gap. *n* columns has a width of $(2n - 1)$gr. 'gr' lengths may be non-integer.

```
float: multicol; width: 3gr;
```

Whereas recognition of the world, the advent of a world in which human beings shall enjoy freedom of speech and belief and freedom from fear and want has been proclaimed as the highest aspiration of the common people,

Whereas recognition of the inherent dignity and of the equal and inalienable rights of all members of the human family is the foundation of freedom, justice and peace in the world,

Whereas disregard and contempt for human rights have resulted in barbarous acts which have outraged the conscience of mankind, and

14

Controlling flow next to floats : 'clear'

▨ Initial value: 'none'   ▨ Applies to: block elements   ▨ Inherited: no

Use the 'clear' property to control the flow of floats to the right and left sides of a specified block.

- none: Floats are not positioned and computes a 'clearance' of an element.
- 'left' : Requires the top border edge of the box be below the bottom outer edge of any left-floating boxes.
- 'right' : Requires the top border edge of the box be below the bottom outer edge of any right-floating boxes.
- 'both' : Requires the top border edge of the box be below the bottom outer edge of any left-floating and right-floating boxes.

Alternative text : '-ah-alttext' ▨

▨ Initial value: "" (the empty string)   ▨ Applies to: `<a>`, `<img>`, and `<svg>`
▨ Inherited: no

The '-ah-alttext' property behaves similarly to the HTML `alt` attribute. It specifies alternative text that is included in Tagged PDF output. (See Tagged PDF (page 156).)

MATHML & SVG GRAPHICS

Equations in MathML are formatted using characters from a mathematical font, such as the STIX fonts, so they are rendered with the same quality as text. SVG graphics are vector images, so they are rendered at the full resolution of the output device.

MathML

A custom-developed engine for Mathematical Markup Language (MathML) 3.0 Second Edition by the W3C is a standard feature of AH Formatter. This makes it possible to render formulas in high quality in PDF.[1]

15

MathML Formatting Examples

If the quadratic formula $ax^2 + bx + c = 0$ produces a solution $D = b^2 - 4ac$,

If $D \geqq 0$, then $x = \dfrac{-b \pm \sqrt{D}}{2a}$

and if $D < 0$, then the solution produces no real numbers.

```
<p>If the quadratic formula
<m:math xmlns:m="http://www.w3.org/1998/Math/MathML"
    xml:lang="">
 <m:mstyle displaystyle="true" scriptminsize="1pt"
      scriptsizemultiplier="0.6">
  <m:mrow>
   <m:msup>
    <m:mrow>
     <m:mi>a</m:mi>
     <m:mo>&#x2062;</m:mo>
     <m:mi>x</m:mi>
    </m:mrow>
    <m:mn>2</m:mn>
   </m:msup>
...
```

---

1 AH Formatter Lite users must purchase the 'AH Formatter MathML Option' separately.

MathML Formatting Examples

If the equation for two straight lines are $y = m_1 x + n_1$ and $y = m_2 x + n_2$

then angle θ formed by the two straight lines is:

$$\tan \theta = \pm \frac{m_2 - m_1}{1 + m_2 m_1} \quad (0° \leqq \theta < 180°)$$

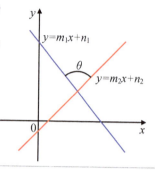

```
<m:math xmlns:m="http://www.w3.org/1998/Math/MathML">
 <m:mstyle displaystyle="true" scriptminsize="1pt"
    scriptsizemultiplier="0.6">
  <m:mo>tan</m:mo>
  <m:mi>θ</m:mi>
  <m:mo>=</m:mo>
  <m:mo>±</m:mo>
  <m:mfrac>
    <m:mrow>
      <m:msub>
        <m:mi>m</m:mi>
        <m:mn>2</m:mn>
      </m:msub>
      <m:mo>-</m:mo>
      <m:msub>
        <m:mi>m</m:mi>
        <m:mn>1</m:mn>
      </m:msub>
    </m:mrow>
    <m:mrow>
      <m:mn>1</m:mn>
      <m:mo>+</m:mo>
      <m:msub>
        <m:mi>m</m:mi>
        <m:mn>2</m:mn>
      </m:msub>
      <m:msub>
        <m:mi>m</m:mi>
        <m:mn>1</m:mn>
      </m:msub>
    </m:mrow>
  </m:mfrac>
  <m:mrow>
    <m:mo lspace="1em">(</m:mo>
    <m:mrow>
      <m:mn>0</m:mn><m:mo>°</m:mo><m:mo>≦</m:mo>
```

```
        <m:mi>θ</m:mi>
        <m:mo>&lt;</m:mo>
        <m:mn>180</m:mn><m:mo>°</m:mo>
      </m:mrow>
      <m:mo>)</m:mo>
    </m:mrow>
  </m:mstyle>
</m:math>
```

Accessibility
Use the `alttext` attribute to specify alternate text for use with screen readers.

```
<m:math xmlns:m="http://www.w3.org/1998/Math/MathML"
    alttext="Formula for the intersection of two lines">…</m:math>
```

SVG Graphics
AH Formatter implements W3C Scalable Vector Graphics (SVG) 1.1 and supports the display of SVG images with a custom-developed engine. This makes it possible to include SVG images in PDF output.

SVG vector graphics   can be embedded.

```
<p>SVG vector graphics
  <s:svg xmlns:s="http://www.w3.org/2000/svg" width="70" height="65"
    viewBox="0 0 70 65">
    <s:g fill-opacity=".5" stroke="black" stroke-width="2">
      <s:circle cx="35" cy="20" r="19" fill="red"/>
      <s:circle cx="49" cy="44" r="19" style="fill: blue;"/>…
    </s:g>
  </s:svg> can be embedded.</p>
```

SVG Examples

Style SVG from document CSS

SVG graphics can use styles that are defined in the CSS style sheet for the document.

Styles from document style sheet

```
@namespace s url(http://www.w3.org/2000/svg);

/* Select element type */
s|circle {
        fill: red;
}
/* Select element type with ID */
circle#circle2 {
        fill: lightblue;
}
/* Select SVG element type with ID */
s|circle#circle3 {
        fill: beige;
}
/* Select SVG element by ID */
#circle4 {
        fill: green;
}
/* Select element type with ID */
circle#circle5 {
        fill: cyan;
}
/* Select element in SVG namespace by ID */
s|#circle6 {
        fill: pink;
}
```

```
<s:svg xmlns:s="http://www.w3.org/2000/svg"
        width="3cm" height="3cm" viewBox="0 0 400 400">
  <s:g style="fill-opacity:0.7; stroke:black;">
    <s:circle cx="6cm" cy="2cm" r="100"
                transform="translate(0,50)" id="circle1"/>
    <s:circle cx="6cm" cy="2cm" r="100"
                transform="translate(70,150)" id="circle2"/>
    <s:circle cx="6cm" cy="2cm" r="100"
```

15

```
                 transform="translate(-70,150)" id="circle3"/>
   </s:g>
</s:svg>
<s:svg xmlns:svg="http://www.w3.org/2000/svg"
          width="3cm" height="3cm" viewBox="0 0 400 400">
  <s:g style="fill-opacity:0.7; stroke:black; stroke-width:0.1cm;">
    <s:circle cx="6cm" cy="2cm" r="100"
                  transform="translate(0,50)" id="circle4"/>
    <s:circle cx="6cm" cy="2cm" r="100"
                  transform="translate(70,150)" id="circle5"/>
    <s:circle cx="6cm" cy="2cm" r="100"
                  transform="translate(-70,150)" id="circle6"/>
   </s:g>
</s:svg>
```

Accessibility

Use '-ah-alttext' in the `style` attribute to specify alternate text for use with screen readers.

```
<s:svg xmlns:s="http://www.w3.org/2000/svg"
    width="70" height="65" viewBox="0 0 70 65"
    style="-ah-alttext: 'Overlapping red, green, and blue circles'">
...
</s:svg>
```

15

COUNTERS

Use the 'counter-increment', 'counter-reset', and 'content' properties to automatically assign a series of numbers to chapter and section elements.

Use the counter name as the value of the 'counter-increment' and 'counter-reset' properties. Specifying a counter name for the 'content' property allows the value of the counter to be used in the content of the '::before' or '::after' pseudo-elements. The counter's value increases each time an element applies 'counter-increment'. The value resets when 'counter-reset' is applied.

```css
body {
    /* reset chapter number counter */
    counter-reset: ChapterNo;
}
h1:before {
    /* add 1 to chapter number counter */
    counter-increment: ChapterNo;
    /* Insert 'Chapter n' before chapter header  (h1)  */
    content: "Chapter " counter(ChapterNo);
}
h1 {
    /* set h1:before and Chapter of h1 */
    string-set: Chapter content(before) content();
    /* reset section number counter */
    counter-reset: SectionNo;
}
h2:before {
    /* add 1 to section counter */
    counter-increment: SectionNo;
    content: counter(ChapterNo) "." counter(SectionNo) " ";
}
h2 { /* set h2:before and Section of h2 */
    string-set: Section content(before) content();
}
@page :left {
    @top-left {
        /* insert chapter title in the running head on the left page */
        content: string(Chapter);
```

```
      }
    }
@page :right {
  @top-right {
    /* insert section title in the running head on the right page */
    content: string(Section);
  }
}
```

Inserting Characters : 'content'

■ Initial value: 'normal'   ■ Applies to: in CSS 2.1, '::before' and '::after' pseudo-elements. (In CSS 3, applies to all elements)   ■ Inherited: no

With CSS 3, you can use the 'content' property to specify a sequence of strings and images as the content of any element. With CSS 2.1, 'content' could only be used with the '::before' and '::after' pseudo-elements to insert a string just before or after an element.

- 'normal' : For an element, this is the element's descendents. For a pseudo-element, this is the same as 'none'.
- 'none' : For an element, this formats the element as if it was empty. For a pseudo-element, this is equivalent to `display: none;`.
- <string> : String to be inserted is written with double or single quotes.
- 'url()' : Specifies the URL of an image file. The content of an element can be made into an image if `content: url(image.png);` is specified.
- 'attr()' : The specified attribute value becomes the 'content' property value.
- 'counter()' : Inserts a counter value.
- 'open-quote' : Inserts the first pair of quotes from the 'quotes' property before the element.
- 'close-quote' : Inserts the second pair of quotes from the 'quotes' property after the element.
- 'no-open-quote' : Does not display a quotation mark but increases the level of nesting of the 'quotes' property by one.
- 'no-close-quote' : Does not display a quotation mark but decreases the level of the nesting of the 'quotes' property by one.

Values other than 'normal' and 'none' may repeat and may be combined in any order.

```
.Chapter h2:before {
  content: "Chapter " counter(ChapterNo) ". ";
}
```

For the 'content()' function that is used with the 'string-set' property, see Variable strings : 'string-set' (page 40).

Incrementing Counters : 'counter-increment'

■Initial value: 'none'　■Applies to: all elements　■Inherited: no

Use the 'counter-increment' property to increase the specified counter value.

- 'none' : Does not alter any counters.
- <custom-ident> : Name of the counter to increment. The value of the specified counter increments by one.
- <custom-ident>, <integer> : Alters the counter value by the integer value. A negative integer decrements the counter value.

More than one counter name, each optionally followed by an integer, may be specified.

```
.Chapter h2 {
    …
    counter-increment: ChapterNo;
    …
}
```

Counter Reset : 'counter-reset'

■Initial value: 'none'　■Applies to: all elements　■Inherited: no

Use 'counter-reset' property to reset the value of the specified counter or counters.

- 'none' : Does not reset count.
- Counter name : Sets the specified counter value to zero.
- Counter name, integer : Sets the counter value to the specified number.

16

```
.Chapter h2 {
    …
    counter-reset: SectionNo footnote;
    …
}
```

Page Counter ▤

Use the 'counter()' function to find the current page and the total number of pages.

```
<p>Number of this page =
    <span style="content: counter(page)"></span>
</p>
<p>Total number of pages in this document=
    <span style="content: counter(pages)"></span>
</p>
```

```
Number of this page = 128
    Total number of pages in this document = 204
```

'counter()' has an optional second argument specifying the counter style (see Counter styles (page 128)). This sets the presentation of the number. If that is omitted, it defaults to 'decimal'.

```
<p>Number of this page =
  <span style="content: counter(page, lower-roman)"></span></p>
<p>Total number of pages in this document=
  <span style="content: counter(pages, upper-roman)"></span></p>
```

```
Number of this page = cxxviii
    Total number of pages in this document = CCIV
```

Counter styles 📑

A "counter style" is the definition and/or implementation of the sequence of numbers, letters, and/or symbols to use to represent a numbering sequence. CSS 1 defined a handful of counter styles based on what HTML allowed on lists. CSS Counter Styles Level 3 defines the '@counter-style' rule, which provides a mechanism for defining custom counter styles. The module also defines a number of counter styles that should all (eventually) be expected to be built into browsers.

The core of a CSS 3 counter style is that it attaches a name to an algorithm for generating string representations of integer counter values. A counter style may also include descriptors for: indicating a prefix and/or suffix to add to the generated values; additional strings to indicate negative numbers, etc. The counter style can be used in the value of the 'list-style-type' property and in the 'counter()' and 'counters()' functions.

The following example shows a 'my-filled-circled-decimal' counter style that is a based on the "filled-circled-decimal" counter style from CSS Counter Styles Level 3. As the name suggests, the counter style uses decimal numbers inside filled circles to represent decimal numbers. The numbers are followed by a space.

```
@counter-style my-filled-circled-decimal {
system: fixed;
symbols: '\2776' '\2777' '\2778' '\2779' '\277a' '\277b' '\277c'
         '\277d' '\277e';
/* symbols: '❶' '❷' '❸' '❹' '❺' '❻' '❼' '❽' '❾'; */
suffix: ' ';
}
ol.my-filled-circled-decimal li {
  list-style-type: my-filled-circled-decimal;  }
```

The 'my-filled-circled-decimal' counter style is used, for example, when numbering the items in an `<ol>`:

```
<ol class="my-filled-circled-decimal">
   <li title="1">Item one</li>
   <li title="2">Item two</li>
</ol>
```

List with 'my-filled-circled-decimal' counter style
❶ Item one   ❷ Item two

Defining Custom Counter Styles : '@counter-style' rule 🅒

The general form of an '@counter-style' rule is:

```
@counter-style <counter-style-name> { <declaration-list> }
```

Counter style names are case-sensitive, However, the names of counter styles that are predefined in CSS Counter Styles Level 3 are matched case insensitively. A counter style name cannot match "none", and "decimal" and "disc" cannot be defined as counter style names.

The following descriptors are allowed in the declaration list:

- 'system' : Specifies which algorithm to use to construct the counter's representation.
- 'negative' : Defines how to alter the representation when the value is negative.
- 'prefix' : Specifies a symbol that is prepended to the marker representation.
- 'suffix' : Specifies a suffix that is appended to the marker representation.
- 'range' : Defines the ranges over which the counter style is defined.
- 'pad' : Specifies a symbol with which to pad counter representations that are not a minimum number of grapheme clusters.
- 'fallback' : Fallback counter style to be used when the current counter style cannot create a representation.
- 'symbols' : Symbols to be used by the marker-construction algorithm.
- 'additive-symbols' : Symbols to be used by an additive marker-construction algorithm.
- 'speak-as' : Describes how to synthesize the spoken form of a counter.[1]

The symbols in the values of the 'negative', 'prefix', 'suffix', 'pad', 'symbols', and 'additive-symbols' descriptors are specified as strings.

---

1 Not implemented by AH Formatter.

Counter algorithm : 'system' descriptor 🗒

■ Initial value: 'symbolic'

Specifies which algorithm to use to construct the counter's representation.

- 'cyclic' : Cycle repeatedly through provided symbols.
- 'numeric' : Interpret the list of counter symbols as digits in a numbering system.
- 'alphabetic' : Interpret the list of symbols as digits to an alphabetic numbering system.
- 'symbolic' : Cycle repeatedly through provided symbols and, on each successive pass, double, triple, etc. the symbols.
- 'additive' : Symbols represent weighted values, and the value of the number is obtained by adding symbols.
- 'fixed' <integer>? : Run through the counter symbols once then fall back to another counter style. <integer>, if present, sets the first symbol value, otherwise the first symbol value is 1.
- 'extends' <counter-style-name> : Use the same algorithm as the specified counter style name.

Formatting negative values : 'negative' descriptor 🗒

■ Initial value: "\2D" ("-" hyphen-minus)

Defines how to alter the representation when the value is negative. The value is one or two symbols. When the value is negative, the first symbol is prepended to the representation and the second symbol, if present, is appended to the representation. For example:

- `negative: "\30DE\30A4\30CA\30B9";` (from japanese-informal) generates "マイナス" ("mainasu") before negative values.
- Financial information frequently uses parentheses to indicate negative values; for example, "(100)" for -100. negative: "(" ")"; generates "(" before negative values and ")" after.

Symbols before the marker : 'prefix' descriptor 🗒

■ Initial value: "" (the empty string)

Specifies a symbol that is prepended to the marker representation. The prefix comes before any negative sign.

Symbols after the marker : 'suffix' descriptor 🗒

■ Initial value: "\2E\20" ("." full stop followed by a space)

Specifies a symbol that is appended to the marker representation. The suffix comes after any negative sign.

16

Range of a counter : 'range' descriptor ▤

▪ Initial value: 'auto'

Defines the ranges over which the counter style is defined. The value is either 'auto' or a comma-separated list of lower and upper bounds of effective ranges. When the value is 'auto', the range is predetermined based on the 'system' value. If the value to be represented is outside all of the ranges of the counter style, the counter style's fallback style is used instead.

Minimum counter width : 'pad' descriptor ▤

▪ Initial value: 0 ""

Specifies a symbol with which to pad counter representations that are not a minimum number of grapheme clusters. The value is an integer and a symbol. When the represention has fewer grapheme clusters than the integer value, the representation is padded with the symbol. Representations that are longer than minimum are not padded.

Fallback counter style : 'fallback' descriptor ▤

▪ Initial value: 'decimal'

Specifies a fallback counter style to be used when the current counter style cannot create a representation.

Symbols for counters : 'symbols' and 'additive-symbols' descriptors ▤

▪ Initial value: n/a

Specifies the symbols used by the marker construction algorithm. 'symbols' is required if 'system' is 'cyclic', 'numeric', 'alphabetic', 'symbolic', or 'fixed', 'additive-symbols' is required if 'system' is 'additive'.

Predefined Counter Styles ▤

CSS Counter Styles Level 3 predefines some counter styles, including some that are noted as commonplace but complicated to represent with '@counter-style'. Ready-made Counter Styles, published by the W3C Internationalization Working Group, provides code snippets for user-defined counter styles for numbering systems used by various cultures around the world. For ease of reference, Ready-made Counter Styles also includes the predefined styles from CSS Counter Styles Level 3.

AH Formatter implements the following predefined styles:[2]

16

Numeric

- arabic-indic
- bengali
- binary
- cambodian
- cjk-decimal
- decimal

---

2 Styles with * are included for backwards-compatibility with an obsolete list-style-type specification.

- devanagari
- fullwidth-decimal
- gujarati
- gurmukhi
- kannada
- khmer
- lao
- lepcha

- lower-hexadecimal
- malayalam
- mongolian
- myanmar
- new-base-60
- octal
- oriya
- persian

- shan
- super-decimal
- tamil
- telugu
- thai
- tibetan
- upper-hexadecimal

Alphabetic

- afar
- agaw
- ari
- blin
- cjk-earthly-branch
- cjk-heavenly-stem
- dizi
- fullwidth-lower-alpha
- 'fullwidth-lower-latin' *
- fullwidth-upper-alpha
- 'fullwidth-upper-latin' *
- gedeo
- gumuz
- hadiyya
- harari
- hindi
- hiragana
- hiragana-iroha
- japanese-formal
- kaffa
- katakana
- katakana-iroha

- kebena
- kembata
- khmer-consonant
- konso
- korean-consonant
- korean-hanja-formal
- korean-hanja-informal
- korean-syllable
- kunama
- lower-alpha
- lower-belorussian
- lower-bulgarian
- lower-greek
- 'lower-latin' *
- lower-macedonian
- lower-oromo-qubee
- lower-russian
- lower-russian-full
- lower-serbo-croatian
- lower-ukrainian
- lower-ukrainian-full
- meen

- oromo
- saho
- sidama
- silti
- thai-alphabetic
- tigre
- upper-alpha
- upper-belorussian
- upper-bulgarian
- 'upper-greek' *
- 'upper-latin' *
- upper-macedonian
- upper-oromo-qubee
- upper-russian
- upper-russian-full
- upper-serbo-croatian
- upper-ukrainian
- upper-ukrainian-full
- wolaita
- yemsa

Additive

- ancient-tamil
- armenian
- georgian
- 'greek' *
- greek-lower-ancient
- greek-lower-modern

- greek-upper-ancient
- greek-upper-modern
- hebrew
- japanese-informal
- korean-hangul-formal
- lower-armenian

- lower-roman
- simple-lower-roman
- simple-upper-roman
- upper-armenian
- upper-roman

16

Symbolic

- lower-alpha-symbolic
- upper-alpha-symbolic

Fixed

- arabic-abjad
- circled-decimal
- circled-ideograph
- circled-katakana
- circled-korean-consonant
- circled-korean-syllable
- circled-lower-latin
- circled-upper-latin
- decimal-leading-zero
- dotted-decimal
- double-circled-decimal
- filled-circled-decimal
- fullwidth-lower-roman
- fullwidth-upper-roman
- maghrebi-abjad
- parenthesized-decimal
- parenthesized-hangul-consonant
- parenthesized-hangul-syllable
- parenthesized-ideograph
- parenthesized-lower-latin
- persian-abjad
- persian-alphabetic

Cyclic

- 'box' *
- 'check' *
- circle
- 'diamond' *
- disc
- 'hyphen' *
- square

Complex

- ethiopic-numeric
- 'kansuji'[3]
- simp-chinese-formal
- simp-chinese-informal
- trad-chinese-formal
- trad-chinese-informal

16

---

3 Converted using '-ah-kansuji-style'. This feature is not available in AH Formatter Lite.

COLOR

When you use CSS with your browser, the colors that you see are from the display emitting light. When the red, green, and blue primary colors combine to make a color, they are additive: the more of each component there is, the lighter the color. This is why #FFF is white (and why white is #FFF).

Conversely, when you print, the colors that you see are from the light that is reflected from the printed surface. When the cyan, magenta, and yellow primaries combine to make a color, they are subtractive: the more of each component there is, the darker the color. 'cmyk(1, 1, 1, 0)' should give black, but in practice, it's closer to a muddy brown. That's one reason why black is added as the fourth color.[1] Using black ink is also less expensive than using a triple quantity of colored inks. Text is typically printed solely in black to avoid problems if the other three inks are not perfectly aligned. A 'richer' black, which might be used for example in a graphic, can be made by applying solid black over one or more other colors.

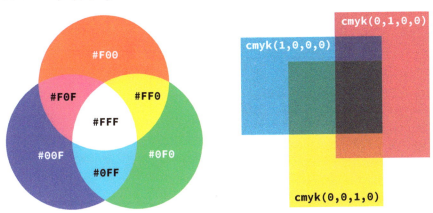

RGB and CMY

---

1 The 'K' in 'CMYK' is from the black printing plate being the 'key' plate against which the other plates are aligned.

The relationship between RGB and CMY was first demonstrated by James Clerk Maxwell around 1860. Put simply, the printing primaries are the secondary colors of the transmitted light primaries, and vice-versa: cyan is blue plus green, or white minus red, and similarly for magenta and yellow. However, as the following figure shows, CMYK printing inks do not have the same gamut (i.e., color range) as the sRGB color space that is used for RGB colors on the web, and neither covers the full gamut of visible light.

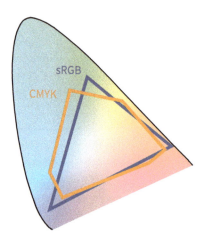

sRGB and CMYK gamuts

These differences between sRGB and CMYK might affect your use of color. Every device or process for printing that you encounter will have a way of representing RGB colors using CMYK. If your paged media will mostly be viewed on screen, possibly with some local printing by end users, then RGB colors may be best. However, if your paged media will be commercially printed, discuss with your printer whether to use RGB or CMYK for images, etc., and who will do the final conversion to CMYK. Preparing images for commercial printing is a complex subject that is beyond the scope of this document.

Text Color : 'color'

■ Initial value: black[2]   ■ Applies to: all elements   ■ Inherited: yes

Use the 'color' property to specify the foreground color of text and border colors. RGB is most commonly used for specifying colors and has three components: red, green, and blue. CMYK are used for print only and has four components: cyan, magenta, yellow, and black. International Color Consortium (ICC) color profiles map between a device-independent color space and the capabilities of a device. RGB and

---

2 The Initial value, 'black', can be changed in the AH Formatter Option Setting File.

ICC colors are converted to CMYK when printing, although they may be retained as RGB or ICC colors in the PDF or other files produced by AH Formatter.

Color can have the following values:

- '#RGB' : Specifies R, G, and B with a one-digit hexadecimal number each. (#5F0 is equivalent to #55FF00)
- '#RRGGBB' : Specifies R, G, and B with a two-digit hexadecimal number each.
- 'rgb(255, 0, 0)' : From the left, specifies R, G, and B with integer values ranging from 0 to 255.
- rgb(100%, 0%, 0%) : From the left, specifies R, G, and B with values ranging from 0% to 100%.
- 'black' (and other colors) : Specifies a color keyword. AH Formatter supports the extended color keywords defined in CSS Color Module Level 3.
- 'cmyk()' : Specifies a CMYK color for four-color process printing.
- 'device-cmyk()' : Same as 'cmyk()'.
- 'rgb-icc()' : Specifies a color in a defined color space.[3] Takes a variable number of arguments (see following).

These examples specify approximately the same red color.

```
em { color: #F00; }                         /* #RGB */
em { color: #FF0000; }                       /* #RRGGBB */
em { color: rgb(255, 0, 0); }                /* integer 0-255 */
em { color: rgb(100%, 0%, 0%); }             /* 0%-100% */
em { color: red; }                           /* color keyword */
em { color: cmyk(0, 0.992, 1, 0); }          /* 0.0-1.0 */
em { color: cmyk(0%, 99.2%, 100%, 0%); }     /* 0%-100% */
em { color: rgb-icc(#CMYK, 0, 0.992, 1, 0); } /* Profile dependent*/
```

If the CSS style sheet will also be used with a browser or with another print media formatter that does not support colors specified as CMYK, then an RGB fallback should be specified before the CMYK color specification:

```
li::marker {
  color: rgb(0, 61, 25);
  color: rgb-icc(#CMYK, 0.9, 0, 0.75, 0.83);
}
```

A formatter that does not understand 'rgb-icc()' will ignore the second 'color' declaration, so the first 'color' declaration will apply. If the declarations were in the reverse order, then the declaration with 'rgb-icc()' would not be used by any formatter.

---

3 'rgb-icc()' is defined in XSL 1.1 and implemented for CSS by AH Formatter.

Color keywords

AH Formatter supports the basic color keywords defined in CSS 2.1 plus the additional extended color keywords defined for CSS 3.

Basic Color Keywords

aqua	aqua	#00FFFF	black	black	#000000
blue	blue	#0000FF	fuchsia	fuchsia	#FF00FF
gray	gray	#808080	green	green	#008000
lime	lime	#00FF00	maroon	maroon	#800000
navy	navy	#000080	olive	olive	#808000
orange	orange	#FFA500	purple	purple	#800080
red	red	#FF0000	silver	silver	#C0C0C0
teal	teal	#008080	white	white	#FFFFFF
yellow	yellow	#FFFF00			

CMYK colors

CMYK colors may be specified with or without a fallback RGB color for use with media that do not support CMYK. When the fallback RGB color is not provided, it is calculated from the CMYK color.

- cmyk(<C>, <M>, <Y>, <K>) : CMYK color with Cyan, Magenta, Yellow, and Black components.
- device-cmyk(<C>, <M>, <Y>, <K>) : Equivalent defined by GCPM.
- rgb-icc(#CMYK, <C>, <M>, <Y>, <K>) : Equivalent.
- rgb-icc(<R>, <G>, <B>, #CMYK, <C>, <M>, <Y>, <K>) : CMYK color with fallback RGB color.

These examples specify the same red color.

```
em { color: cmyk(0, 0.992, 1, 0); }                      /* 0.0-1.0 */
em { color: cmyk(0%, 99.2%, 100%, 0%); }                 /* 0%-100% */
em { color: device-cmyk(0, 0.992, 1, 0); }               /* 0.0-1.0 only */
em { color: rgb-icc(#CMYK, 0, 0.992, 1, 0); }            /* 0.0-1.0 */
em { color: rgb-icc(#CMYK, 0%, 99.2%, 100%, 0%); }       /* 0%-100% */
em { color: rgb-icc(255, 0, 0, #CMYK, 0, 0.992, 1, 0); }
                                                         /* RGB 0-255 */
em { color: rgb-icc(1.0, 0, 0, #CMYK, 0%, 99.2%, 100%, 0%); }
                                                         /* RGB 0.0-1.0 */
```

17

100% black : 'k100'

Many printing or publishing services either require or recommend that text is printed as 100% black ink with no cyan, magenta, or yellow components; that is, as 'cmyk(0, 0, 0, 1)'. The 'black' color keyword is equivalent to 'rgb(0, 0, 0)' in the RGB colorspace. There is no guarantee that 'black' will be converted to 'cmyk(0, 0, 0, 1)' when RGB colors are converted to CMYK for printing. As a convenience, AH Formatter supports 'k100' as a color keyword that is equivalent to 'cmyk(0, 0, 0, 1)'. The effect of specifying 'k100' instead of as 'black' will depend upon the RGB-to-CMYK conversion and on the printing device. Any effect is likely to be more apparent at smaller point sizes.

Opacity

RGB and CMYK colors can also be specified with an 'alpha' component that determines the opacity of the color. It is not possible to use an 'alpha' component with a named color.

These examples specify approximately the same red color with 50% (or near 50%) opacity.

```
em { color: #F008; }                              /* #RGBA */
em { color: #FF000088; }                          /* #RRGGBBAA */
em { color: rgba(255, 0, 0, 0.5); }               /* Opacity 0.0-1.0 */
em { color: rgba(255, 0, 0, 50%); }               /* Opacity 0%-100% */
em { color: rgba(100%, 0%, 0%, 0.5); }            /* Opacity 0.0-1.0 */
em { color: rgba(100%, 0%, 0%, 50%); }            /* Opacity 0%-100% */
em { color: cmyka(0, 0.992, 1, 0, 0.5); }         /* Opacity 0.0-1.0 */
em { color: cmyka(0, 0.992, 1, 0, 50%); }         /* Opacity 0%-100% */
em { color: cmyka(0%, 99.2%, 100%, 0%, 0.5); }    /* Opacity 0.0-1.0 */
em { color: cmyka(0%, 99.2%, 100%, 0%, 50%); }    /* Opacity 0%-100% */
```

17

Opacity levels							
#F00F	#F00E	#F00D	#F00C	#F00B	#F00A	#F009	#F008
#F007	#F006	#F005	#F004	#F003	#F002	#F001	#F000

'rgb-icc()'

The 'rgb-icc()' color function provides additional ways to specify colors, including:
- rgb-icc(#CMYK, 0.5, 0.5, 0.5, 0) : CMYK color.
- rgb-icc(#Grayscale, 0.5) : Grayscale
- rgb-icc(#Separation, 'Name') : Spot color.
- rgb-icc(#Registration) : Print with the same intensity on all separations.
- rgb-icc(#Separation, 'All') : Same as rgb-icc(#Registration).

Grayscale

Grayscale (monochrome) colors can be specified with rgb-icc(#Grayscale, <Scale>), optionally with extra parameters specifying a fallback RGB color for use with devices that cannot display the grayscale color.

These examples specify 50% gray.

```
em { color: rgb-icc(#Grayscale, 0.5); }
                        /* 0.0 (black) to 1.0 (white) */
em { color: rgb-icc(#Grayscale, 50%); }
                        /* 0% (black) to 100% (white) */
em { color: rgb-icc(128, 128, 128, #Grayscale, 0.5); }
                        /* RGB fallback color */
em { color: rgb-icc(50%, 50%, 50%, #Grayscale, 0.5); }
                        /* RGB fallback color */
```

Grayscale levels											
0.0	0.1	0.2	0.3	0.4	0.5	0.6	0.7	0.8	0.9	1.0

PANTONE® spot colors

When you have the AH Formatter PANTONE® Option[4] you can specify more than 1,000 PANTONE® colors by name and have them print as a spot color or be converted into the correct RGB or CMYK for rendering or printing.

These examples specify the same PANTONE® color at either 100% or 50% tint.

```
/* Name and tint */
em { color: rgb-icc(#Separation, 'PANTONE 627 PC', 1.0); }
/* Tint 0.0 to 1.0 */
em { color: rgb-icc(#Separation, 'PANTONE 627 PC', 0.5); }
/* Tint 0% to 100% */
em { color: rgb-icc(#Separation, 'PANTONE 627 PC', 50%); }
/* Assume 1.0 tint */
em { color: rgb-icc(#Separation, 'PANTONE 627 PC'); }
/* With CMYK equivalent. */
em { color: rgb-icc(#Separation, 'PANTONE 627 PC', 1,
                90%, 0%, 75%, 83%); }
/* With RGB equivalent. */
em { color: rgb-icc(0, 91, 25, #Separation, 'PANTONE 627 PC'); }
/* With both RGB and CMYK equivalents. */
em { color: rgb-icc(0, 91, 25, #Separation, 'PANTONE 627 PC', 1,
                90%, 0%, 75%, 83%); }
```

17

4 The 'AH Formatter PANTONE® Option' must be purchased separately.

Tint levels

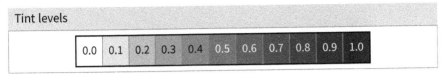

0.0	0.1	0.2	0.3	0.4	0.5	0.6	0.7	0.8	0.9	1.0

When the formatted document is commercially printed, each PANTONE® color can have a separate printing with the specific ink for that PANTONE® color. The grayscale levels on the separation for each PANTONE® color correspond to the level of tint to apply.

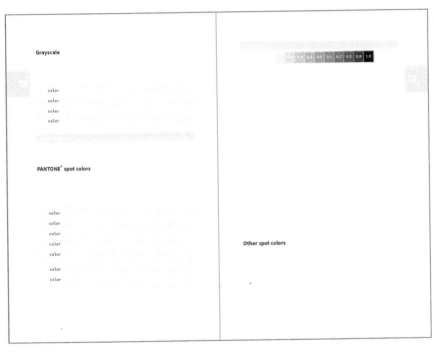

Greyscale levels on the separation correspond to the level of tint to apply

Other spot colors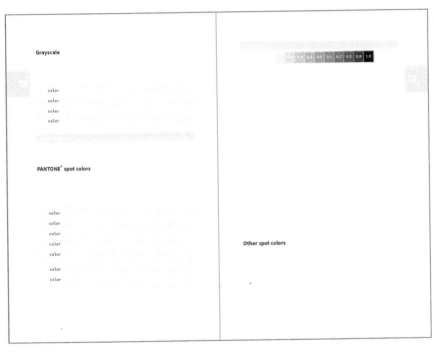

Spot colors can be used without the AH Formatter PANTONE® Option. However, it is necessary to provide one or both of the equivalent RGB and CMYK colors for use with media that does not support separations for spot colors. If either of the RGB or CMYK equivalent is omitted, it is calculated from the components of the other equivalent color.

- rgb-icc(<R>, <G>, <B>, #Separation, <Name>, <Tint, <C>, <M>, <Y>, <K>) : Spot color with name, tint, and both CMYK and RGB fallback colors.

- rgb-icc(<R>, <G>, <B>, #Separation, <Name>, <Tint) : Spot color with name, tint, and RGB fallback color.
- rgb-icc(<R>, <G>, <B>, #Separation, <Name>, <Tint) : Spot color with name and RGB fallback color.
- rgb-icc(#Separation, <Name>, <Tint, <C>, <M>, <Y>, <K>) : Spot color with name, tint, and CMYK fallback color.

Similarly to PANTONE® colors, when the formatted document is commercially printed, each CMYK spot color can have a separate printing with the specific ink for that color. The grayscale levels in the separation for each color correspond to the level of tint to apply.

17

BORDERS & BACKGROUND

Any element, such as `<p>`, that can generate a box can specify its borders using the border-related properties. These set the borders' thickness, color, line type (style), and rounding of corners as well as adding of shadows to the borders. Additionally, 'background-color' sets the background color of the object and 'background-image' and related properties sets an image or images to render over the background color.

Border Thickness : 'border-width'

■ Initial value: 'medium' ■ Applies to: all elements ■ Inherited: no
One to four component values that set the border widths for all four sides.

'thin' : A thin border.

'medium' : A medium border

'thick' : A thick border.

<length> : an explicit length. For example, `border-width: 2pt;`. Cannot be negative.

The individual border width properties are 'border-top-width', 'border-right-width', 'border-bottom-width', and 'border-left-width'. Their initial values are all 'medium'.

Border Color : 'border-color'

■ Initial value: current 'color' value ■ Applies to: all elements ■ Inherited: no
One to four component values that set the border color for all four sides.
- <color> : A color. See 17. COLOR (page 135) for details.
- 'transparent' : The border is transparent, though it may have width.

The individual border color properties are 'border-top-color', 'border-right-color', 'border-bottom-color', and 'border-left-color'. Their initial values are the current value of the 'color' property.

Border Style : 'border-style'

■ Initial value: 'none'   ■ Applies to: all elements   ■ Inherited: no
One to four component values that set the border styles for all four sides. The following border style values may be used.

'none' : No borders. (thickness = 0)

'hidden' : Hides border.

'solid' : Solid line.

'double' : Double line.

'dotted' : Dotted line.

'dashed' : Dashed line.

'dot-dash' : Dot-dash line.

'dot-dot-dash' : Two-dot chain line.

'wave' : Wave line.

'groove' : Border looks as though it is carved into the canvas.

'ridge' : Border looks as though it is coming out of the canvas.

'inset' : The content looks as though it is sunken into the canvas.

'outset' : The content looks as though it is coming out of the canvas.

'hidden' is the same as 'none' except within tables with `border-collapse: collapse;`. See Whether to merge adjacent borders : 'border-collapse' (page 74).

The individual border style properties are 'border-top-style', 'border-right-style', 'border-bottom-style', and 'border-left-style'. Their initial values are all 'none'.

Per-side Border Properties : 'border-top' / 'border-right' / 'border-bottom' / 'border-left'

■ Initial value: see individual properties   ■ Applies to: all elements
■ Inherited: no

Each property specifies the width, style, and color of the top, right, bottom, or left border of a box.

Border Shorthand : 'border'

■ Initial value: see individual properties   ■ Applies to: all elements
■ Inherited: no

Specifies the width, style, and color of all four borders of a box.

Rounded Corners : 'border-radius'

■ Initial value: 0   ■ Applies to: all elements   ■ Inherited: no

Specify the 'border-radius' property to make rounded corners.

```
<p style="border-radius: 18pt; /* rounded corner radius */
          border: solid green;
          padding: 6pt;">Specifies 'border-radius'...
```

Specifies 'border-radius' (rounding rule).

The radii of each corner can be set individually using 'border-top-left-radius', 'border-top-right-radius', 'border-bottom-left-radius', and 'border-bottom-right-radius'.

```
<p style="border-top-left-radius: 2mm;        /* top-left */
          border-top-right-radius: 5mm;       /* top-right */
          /* bottom-right (horizontal and vertical direction) */
          border-bottom-right-radius: 4cm 2cm;
          /* bottom-left (horizontal and vertical direction) */
          border-bottom-left-radius: 2cm 1cm;
          border: thin solid;
          background-color: lime;
          padding: 5mm;">...
```

18

Radii of each of the four corners can be set individually. Rounded corners can also generate an ellipse.

Box Shadow : 'box-shadow'

■ Initial value: 'none' ■ Applies to: all elements ■ Inherited: no

Adds a shadow to a box when 'box-shadow' property is specified with the horizontal and vertical shadow length and shadow color.

```
<p style="box-shadow: 8pt 6pt silver;
          border: solid 1pt black; padding: 6pt">…
```

Sets Box-shadow (Shadowed boxes).

```
<p style="box-shadow: -8pt -6pt orange, 8pt 6pt blue;
          border-radius: 10pt; padding: 6pt">…
```

Multiple shadows can be specified. 'border-radius' also affects 'box-shadow'.

```
<p><span style="box-shadow: 8pt 6pt silver; border: solid 0.5pt;">
  Box shadows do not affect margins.</span></p>
```

Box shadows do not affect margins. Ensure that the box shadows do not give an unwanted effect of apparently changing the space between blocks.

Box shadows do not affect margins.
Section Title

Box shadows do not affect margins.
Section Title

Backgrounds

Every CSS box has a background color. The default value of the 'background-color' property is 'transparent', so while the background color is always present, it is not always visible.

A CSS box may also have one or more background images that are rendered above the background color but below the rendered content. There are multiple properties for specifying background images and their positions. The properties are described for a single background image, then usage for multiple images is shown in Multiple background images (page 154).

18

Background color : 'background-color'

Initial value: 'transparent'   Applies to: all elements   Inherited: no

Use 'background-color' to set the background color. The initial value, 'transparent', lets the contents of the parent element (underlying colors) show through.

Background color applies to the content, padding, and border of an ordinary box model. Margins are always transparent, and the background color does not apply to them. The background color is drawn behind any background images.

- The background color is applied to the entire surface of a page box.
- With respect to boxes of root elements, the background color is applied to content, padding, border, and margin.
- <color> : A color. See 17. COLOR (page 135) for details.
- 'transparent' : The border is transparent, though it may have width.

Background image : 'background-image'

Initial value: 'none'   Applies to: all elements   Inherited: no

Use 'background-image' to set the background image of an element. The image, if it is available, shows on top of the background color.

- 'none' : No image is used.
- <uri> : Location of an image to render.

Resolution of a background image : '-ah-background-image-resolution'

Initial value: 'normal'   Applies to: all elements   Inherited: no

Use '-ah-background-image-resolution' to set the resolution of background image that either does not have an intrinsic resolution or should be rendered at a different resolution to its default.

- 'normal' : Use the default resolution of the system and ignore the actual resolution of the image.
- 'from-image' : Use the actual resolution of the image. If the image does not have an intrinsic resolution, this is the same as 'normal'.
- <dpi> : Use the specified resolution and ignore the actual resolution of the image.

Background image content type : '-ah-background-image-content-type'

Initial value: 'auto'   Applies to: all elements   Inherited: no

Use '-ah-background-image-content-type' to set the content type for a background image that would not otherwise be handled correctly.

- 'auto' : Automatically determine the content type.
- <string> : Content type to use for the image.

Background image size : 'background-size'

■ Initial value: 'auto' ■ Applies to: all elements ■ Inherited: no

'background-size' specifies the size of the background image. An explicit size for one or both of the horizontal and vertical dimensions may be specified, or the 'contain' or 'cover' keyword may be specified to automatically scale the image.

- 'contain' : Scale the image, while preserving its aspect ratio, to the largest size such that the image fits within the background positioning area.
- 'center' : Scale the image, while preserving its aspect ratio, to the smallest size such that both its width and its height cover the background positioning area.
- <length-percentage> | 'auto']{1,2} : The first value gives the width of the image. The second value, if present, gives the height. Any missing value is treated as 'auto'.

An 'auto' value is resolved using the aspect ratio of the image and its other dimension or, failing that, by treating it as 100%. If both values are 'auto', then the intrinsic size of the image should be used. If the image has an intrinsic size in only one dimension, then the other dimension is treated as 'auto'. If the image has neither an intrinsic width or intrinsic height, then its size is determined as for 'contain'.

'background-size' examples

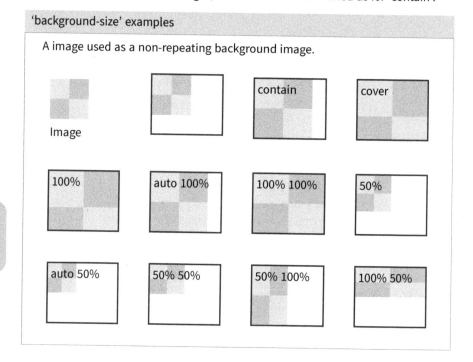

18

Background image position : 'background-position'

■ Initial value: 0% 0%　■ Applies to: all elements　■ Inherited: no

'background-position' specifies the initial position of the background image, if one has been specified. One or both of a horizontal and vertical position may be specified. If one value is specified, then the second value is assumed to be 'center'. If at least one value is not a keyword, then the first value represents the horizontal position and the second, if present, represents the vertical position.

A keyword for horizontal position plus a keyword for vertical position may be specified in either order, but not a keyword plus a length or percentage. For example, top left and left top are both valid, and left 0 is also valid, but 0 left is not valid.

Horizontal position may be specifed as:
- <percentage> : A percentage X aligns the point X% across the image with the point X% across the element's padding box.
- <length> : horizontal offset of the top left corner of the image from the top left corner of the element's padding box.
- 'left' : Equivalent to 0%.
- 'center' : Equivalent to 50%.
- 'right' : Equivalent to 100%.

Vertical position may be specifed as:
- <percentage> : A percentage X aligns the point X% down the image with the point X% down the element's padding box.
- <length> : vertical offset of the top left corner of the image from the top left corner of the element's padding box.
- 'top' : Equivalent to 0%.
- 'center' : Equivalent to 50%.
- 'bottom' : Equivalent to 100%.

Negative percentage and length values are allowed.

The following figure illustrates the effect of position keywords and percentage values. The alignment point for each square image is at the intersection of the thick lines in the square.

18

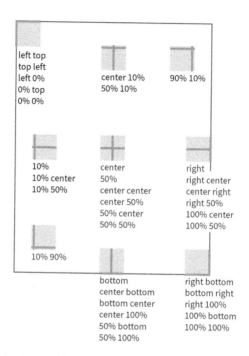

left top
top left
left 0%
0% top
0% 0%

center 10%
50% 10%

90% 10%

10%
10% center
10% 50%

center
50%
center center
center 50%
50% center
50% 50%

right
right center
center right
right 50%
100% center
100% 50%

10% 90%

bottom
center bottom
bottom center
center 100%
50% bottom
50% 100%

right bottom
bottom right
right 100%
100% bottom
100% 100%

Example background images positioned using keywords or percentages

Repetitions of a background image : 'background-repeat'

■ Initial value: 'repeat'   ■ Applies to: all elements   ■ Inherited: no

'background-repeat' specifies whether, and how, a background image is tiled. Tiling is applied after 'background-size' and 'background-position' have been applied.

In CSS3, 'background-repeat' is defined in terms of four keywords. These keywords may be specified once or twice, in any combination. When there are two keywords, the first keyword applies to the horizontal direction and the second applies to the vertical direction.

- 'repeat' : Image is repeated in this direction as often as needed to cover the background painting area.
- 'space' : Image is repeated in this direction as often as will fit in the background positioning area and then the images are spaced out to fill the area. The first and last images touch the edges of the area.
- 'round' : Image is repeated in this direction as often as will fit without being clipped.
- 'no-repeat' : Image is not repeated in this direction.

The single-keyword values, including the 'repeat-x' and 'repeat-y' keywords from CSS2, are defined in terms of those keywords:

18

- 'repeat-x' : Image is repeated horizontally only. Equivalent to `repeat no-repeat`.
- 'repeat-y' : Image is repeated vertically only. Equivalent to `no-repeat repeat`.
- 'repeat' : Image is repeated both horizontally and vertically. Equivalent to `repeat repeat`.
- 'space' : Equivalent to `space space`.
- 'round' : Equivalent to `round round`.
- 'no-repeat' : Image is not repeated: only one copy is drawn. Equivalent to `no-repeat no-repeat`.

AH Formatter supports an additional keyword as the 'background-repeat' value:
- 'paginate' : When the background image is a PDF file, use successive pages of the PDF as the background of successive pages of the current document. Applies only to the background of an '@page' rule and only when the output is PDF. This feature is not available in AH Formatter Lite.

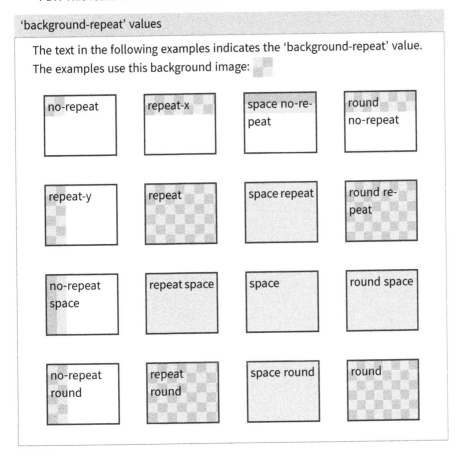

'background-repeat' values

The text in the following examples indicates the 'background-repeat' value. The examples use this background image:

18

Background positioning area : 'background-origin'

■ Initial value: 'padding-box' ■ Applies to: all elements ■ Inherited: no

'background-origin' specifies the box within which the background image is positioned. Position `0` `0` (which is also position `0%` `0%`) is at the top-left of the positioning area. Position `100%` `100%` is at the bottom-right of the positioning area.

- 'border-box' : Position is relative to the border box.
- 'padding-box' : Position is relative to the padding box.
- 'content-box' : Position is relative to the content box.

'background-origin' affects the placement of the background image, but it does not affect clipping of the image (or of repetitions of the image). 'background-clip' specifies the area to which the background image is clipped.

In the following examples, the inner, dotted border indicates the extent of the content box of the outer block, and the text indicates the 'background-origin' value. All background images are the same size.

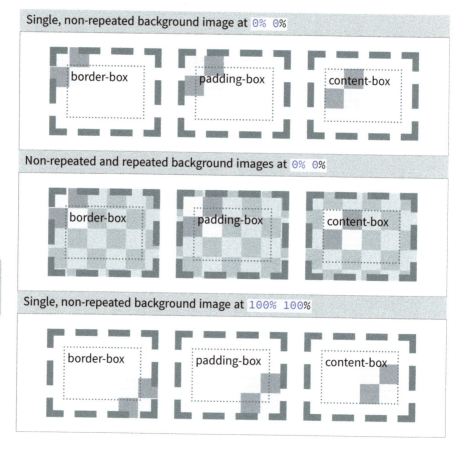

18

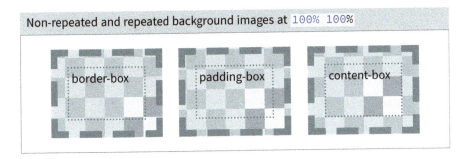
Non-repeated and repeated background images at `100% 100%`

Background painting area : 'background-clip'

■ Initial value: 'padding-box' ■ Applies to: all elements except the root element
■ Inherited: no

'background-clip' specifies the area within which the background is painted.

- 'border-box' : Clipped to the border box.
- 'padding-box' : Clipped to the padding box.
- 'content-box' : Clipped to the content box.

'background-clip' has no effect on the root element.

Depending on the 'background-origin' and 'background-position' values, the specified 'background-clip' value may cause one or more repetitions of the background image to be clipped. In the following examples, the dotted border indicates the extent of the content box of the outer block, and the text indicates the 'background-clip' value. All background images are the same size.

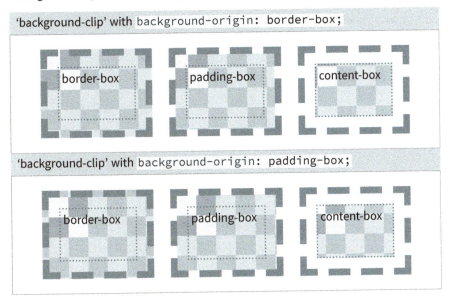

'background-clip' with `background-origin: border-box;`

'background-clip' with `background-origin: padding-box;`

18

border-box   padding-box   content-box

Background Image On Every Page : 'background-attachment'

■ Initial value: 'scroll'   ■ Applies to: all elements   ■ Inherited: no

'background-attachment' specifies whether a background image is replicated on every page.

- 'fixed' : The background image is replicated on every page.
- 'scroll' : The background image does not repeat across pages.
- 'local' : The background image does not repeat across pages.

Multiple background images

Multiple background images separated by commas may be specified as the value of the 'background-image' property. All of the other background image-related properties may also be specified as multiple comma-separated values. Each value in sequence applies to the corresponding 'background-image' image. If a property contains fewer comma-separated values than there are background images, then the last specified value is used for the remaining images.

```
background-image: url(images/background-size-background-darker.svg),
                  url(images/background-size-background.svg);
background-repeat: no-repeat, repeat;
```

Background shorthand : 'background'

■ Initial value: see individual   ■ Applies to: all elements   ■ Inherited: no

The 'background' shorthand specifies the background images and background color in one declaration. All of the properties for one background image are specified together, and the sets of properties for each image are separated by commas. The optional last component of the 'background' value is the background color.

```
'background'      = [ <bg-layer>, ]* <final-bg-layer>
<bg-layer>        = <background-image> || <background-repeat> ||
                    <background-position> [ / <background-size> ]? ||
                    <background-attachment> || <background-clip> ||
                    <background-origin>
<final-bg-layer> = <bg-layer> || <background-color>
```

18

PDF OUTPUT

Portable Document Format (PDF) is the most popular output format for paged media. PDF is useful for distributing formatted documents to users, for exchanging print-ready documents with a printing service, and for long-term preservation of formatted documents. A PDF document may include information about its logical structure that can be used by screen readers.

CSS 3 defines properties that may be used for PDF bookmarks. AH Formatter provides multiple extensions for taking advantage of PDF features.

PDF Versions

The PDF specification has gone through multiple versions since 1993. Each release has added new features. All non-deprecated features in a PDF version are also included in subsequent versions. A PDF file includes a header identifying the PDF version to which it conforms. A PDF reader will attempt to read any PDF file, even if the file's version is more recent than the version that the reader implements.

Version	Year	Acrobat Reader
1.3	2000	4.0
1.4	2001	5.0
1.5	2003	6.0

Version	Year	Acrobat Reader
1.6	2004	7.0
1.7	2008	8
2.0	2017	–

There are also specialized subsets of PDF that have been standardized by ISO.[1] Some of these have multiple versions that are each based on a specific PDF version.

- PDF/X : "PDF for Exchange".
- PDF/A : "PDF for Archiving".
- PDF/E : "PDF for Engineering".
- PDF/VT : "PDF for exchange of variable data and transactional (VT) printing".
- PDF/UA : "PDF for Universal Accessibility".

19

---

1 AH Formatter does not generate either PDF/E or PDF/VT.

Tagged PDF

"Tagged PDF" is not a separate PDF specification. It refers to PDF that includes additional information about the logical structure of the document. Tagged PDF was first defined in PDF 1.4.

The text, graphics, and images in Tagged PDF can be extracted and reused for other purposes. For example, to make content accessible to users with visual impairments. PDF/UA files are Tagged PDF files that also conform to additional requirements.

AH Formatter embeds PDF tags ('StructElem') for HTML/CSS elements and pseudo-elements as shown in the following table:

HTML element	PDF element	HTML element	PDF element
html	Document	caption	Caption
div	Div	table	Table
h1	H1	tr	TR
h2	H2	td	TD
h3	H3	th	TH
h4	H4	thead	THead
h5	H5	tfoot	TFoot
h6	H6	tbody	TBody
p	P	ruby	Ruby
ul	L	rb	RB
ol	L	rt	RT
li	LI	span	Span
li::marker	Lbl	img	Figure
dl	L	a[href]	Link
dt	Lbl	other block elements	Div
dd	LBody	other inline elements	Span
blockquote	BlockQuote		

Custom PDF Tag name : '-ah-pdftag'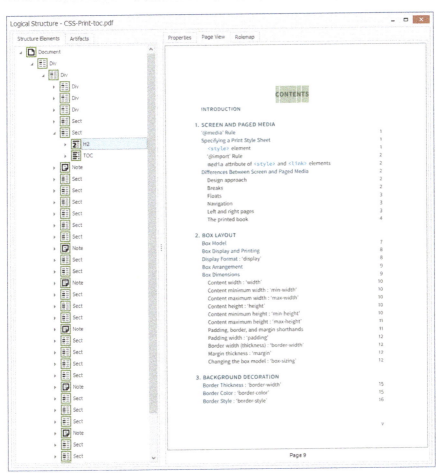

■ Initial value: Empty string　■ Applies to: all elements　■ Inherited: no

String to use as the PDF Tag name for the current element when generating Tagged PDF. If the provided name is not one of the standard PDF Tag names, the role map in the generated PDF will include a mapping from the name to the default PDF Tag name that AH Formatter would generate for the current element. If the provided name is one of the standard PDF Tag names, the name will be used as-is.

```
div.TOC {
    page-break-before: right;
    page: TOC;
    -ah-pdftag: 'Sect';
}
```

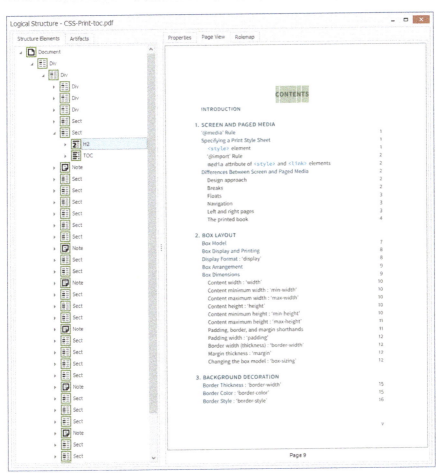

<div class="TOC"> is tagged as 'Sect' in the PDF

PDF/X

PDF/X, defined in ISO 15930, is a subset of PDF that is intended for prepress graphics exchange.[2] The intention is that all of the information required for printing is included in the PDF file.

AH Formatter supports multiple PDF/X variants:

- PDF/X-1a:2001 (ISO 15930-1:2001) – Based on PDF 1.3.
- PDF/X-3:2002 (ISO 15930-3:2002) – Based on PDF 1.3.
- PDF/X-1a:2003 (ISO 15930-4:2003) – A subset of PDF/X-3:2003 that is based on PDF 1.4.
- PDF/X-2:2003 (ISO 15930-5:2003) – A superset of PDF/X-3:2003 that is based on PDF 1.4.
- PDF/X-3:2003 (ISO 15930-6:2003) – Based on PDF 1.4.
- PDF/X-4:2010 (ISO 15930-7:2008) – Based on PDF 1.6.

Main features of supported PDF/X variants.

Requirement	PDF/X-1a	PDF/X-2	PDF/X-3	PDF/X-4
All fonts must be embedded	yes	yes	yes	yes
The output intent must be specified	yes	yes	yes	yes
ICC profiles specified as the output intent must be embedded	no	no	no	yes
Supports CMYK, Spot color	yes	yes	yes	yes
Supports Grayscale	yes	yes	yes	yes
Supports RGB	no	yes	yes	yes
Supports transparency	no	no	no	yes
Supports PDFs with encryption; a password must not be set, and the restriction against printing and the restriction against changing must not be enabled	no	no	no	no
PDF can contain links or annotations, etc. in the print area	no	no	no	no

19

---

2 PDF/X output is not available with AH Formatter Lite.

PDF/A

PDF/A, defined in ISO 19005, is a subset of PDF that is intended for long-term preservation of electronic documents.[3]

Features of supported PDF/A variants

Requirement	PDF/A-1a	PDF/A-1b	PDF/A-2a	PDF/A-2b	PDF/A-2u	PDF/A-3a	PDF/A-3b	PDF/A-3u
All fonts must be embedded	yes	yes	yes	yes	yes	yes	yes	yes
ICC profiles must be embedded	yes	yes	yes	yes	yes	yes	yes	yes
Files must be tagged	yes	no	yes	no	no	yes	no	no
Files must include XMP metadata	yes	yes	yes	yes	yes	yes	yes	yes
Files may include encryption	no	no	no	no	no	no	no	no
Files may include LZW Compression	no	no	no	no	no	no	no	no
Files may include Transparent images	no	no	yes	yes	yes	yes	yes	yes
Files may refer to external content	no	no	no	no	no	no	no	no
Files may include JavaScript	no	no	no	no	no	no	no	no
Unicode must be used for text	no	no	yes	no	yes	yes	no	yes
Any files other than PDF/A can be embedded	no	no	no	no	no	yes	yes	yes

19

---

3 PDF/A output is not available with AH Formatter Lite.

PDF/UA

PDF/UA, defined in ISO 14289-1, is the specification intended for improving the accessibility of PDF based on the ISO 32000-1 (PDF 1.7) specification.[4]

The main features of PDF/UA are:

- Contents must be tagged in logical reading order.
- Meaningful graphics, annotations and numerical formulas must include alternate text descriptions.

  Alternate text descriptions for graphics or numerical formulas can be specified by the '-ah-alttext' property, links can be specified by the '-ah-annotation-contents' property.

- Security settings must allow assistive technology to have access to the content.
- Including bookmarks in the PDF/UA is recommended.
- Annotations, links and multimedia may be included.
- The language of the document must be specified.
- All fonts must be embedded.

Matterhorn Protocol

The Matterhorn Protocol, published by the PDF Association, is a checklist of all the ways that it is possible for a PDF to not conform to PDF/UA. The Matterhorn Protocol document consists of 31 Checkpoints comprised of 136 Failure Conditions. Some failure conditions can be checked programmatically, but others require human review.

Checkpoint 15: Tables

Index	Failure Condition	Section	Type	How	See
15-001	A row has a header cell, but that header cell is not tagged as a header.	UA1:7.5-1	Object	Human	-
15-002	A column has a header cell, but that header cell is not tagged as a header.	UA1:7.5-1	Object	Human	-
15-003	In a table not organized with Headers attributes and IDs, a TH cell does not contain a Scope attribute.	UA1:7.5-2	Object	Machine	-
15-004	Content is tagged as a table for information that is not organized in rows and columns.	UA1:7.5-3	Object	Human	-
15-005	A given cell's header cannot be unambiguously determined.	UA1:7.5-2	Object	Human	01-006

Matterhorn Protocol failure conditions for tables

PAC 3 PDF/UA checker

PDF Accessibility Checker 3 (PAC 3)[5] by Access For All is a freeware utility for Windows that checks PDF files for PDF/UA conformance. The program implements the Matterhorn Protocol checks. When you open a PDF file in PAC 3, the program runs its

---

4 PDF/UA output is not available with AH Formatter Lite.
5 http://www.access-for-all.ch/en/pdf-lab/536-pdf-accessibility-checker-pac-3.html

checks and shows a summary of the results. Since there is no interactive checking, the program can only warn about some of the failure conditions that require human checking.

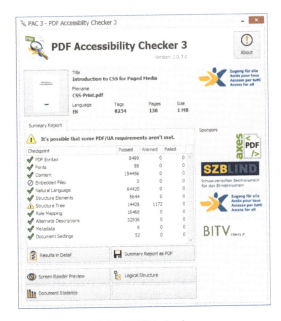

PAC 3 PDF/UA checker

Document Properties ▰

This extension uses custom `<meta>` elements, for example:

```
<meta name="document-title" content="The document title"/>
<meta name="subject" content="The document subject"/>
<meta name="author" content="The author"/>
<meta name="keywords" content="Comma, separated, keywords, list"/>
...
```

`<meta>` with the following name values provide information that is stored in the document catalog in the PDF.[6]
- 'document-title' : Title of the document.
- 'subject' : Subject of the document.
- 'author' : Name of the person who created the document.
- 'author-title' : Title or some other information about the author.
- 'description-writer' : Author of the document description.

---

6 'author-title', 'description-writer', 'copyright-status', 'copyright-notice', 'copyright-info-url', and 'xmp' are not available with AH Formatter Lite.

- 'keywords' : Comma-separated list of keywords.
- 'copyright-status' : Copyright status. Must be 'Unknown', 'Copyrighted', or 'PublicDomain'.
- 'copyright-notice' : Copyright information.
- 'copyright-info-url' : URL of the copyright information.
- 'xmp' : URL of an XMP containing property information.

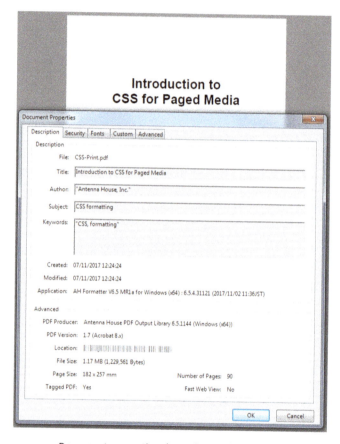

Document properties shown by Acrobat Reader

Extensible Metadata Platform (XMP)

XMP is a standard XML format for representing metadata about a file or image. It was originally developed by Adobe, and it is now also ISO 16684-1:2012. Because there is a standard, the XMP, for example, that is embedded in a photo taken by a digital camera can be altered or augmented by the photo-editing program that edits the image. Also, for example, the XMP from every image in a PDF file could be included in the XMP that is embedded in the PDF file.

The XMP standard itself is based, in part, on other metadata standards such as Dublin Core and RDF.

Any XMP file that passes the sanity check implemented in AH Formatter may be embedded in the PDF that AH Formatter generates.

A portion of the XMP extracted from a PDF file follows, and the following figure shows the same XMP as presented by Acrobat.

```
<?xpacket begin="" id="W5M0MpCehiHzreSzNTczkc9d"?>
<x:xmpmeta xmlns:x="adobe:ns:meta/">
<rdf:RDF xmlns:rdf="http://www.w3.org/1999/02/22-rdf-syntax-ns#">
<rdf:Description rdf:about=""
    xmlns:xapMM="http://ns.adobe.com/xap/1.0/mm/">
<xapMM:DocumentID>uuid:4841192B-77AD-0B4B-BD43-8DF3BDE3A5EA
</xapMM:DocumentID>
<xapMM:VersionID>1</xapMM:VersionID>
<xapMM:RenditionClass>default</xapMM:RenditionClass>
</rdf:Description>
<rdf:Description rdf:about=""
    xmlns:pdf="http://ns.adobe.com/pdf/1.3/">
    <pdf:Producer>Antenna House PDF Output Library 6.5.1216 (Windows
    (x64))</pdf:Producer>
<pdf:Keywords>"CSS, formatting"</pdf:Keywords>
<pdf:Trapped>False</pdf:Trapped>
</rdf:Description>
<rdf:Description rdf:about=""
    xmlns:xap="http://ns.adobe.com/xap/1.0/">
    <xap:CreatorTool>AH Formatter V6.5 MR3 for Windows (x64) :
    6.5.6.31956 (2018/02/02 12:52JST)</xap:CreatorTool>
<xap:ModifyDate>2018-02-25T16:38:45Z</xap:ModifyDate>
<xap:CreateDate>2018-02-25T16:38:45Z</xap:CreateDate>
</rdf:Description>
...
```

19

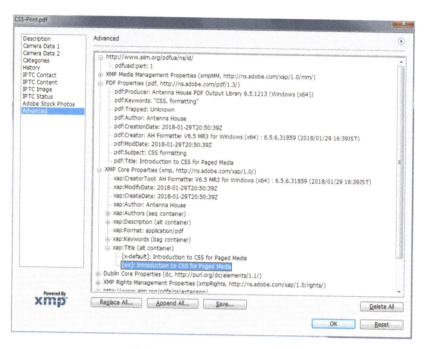

XMP properties viewed in Acrobat

Page Display

`<meta>` with the following name values control how the PDF is displayed when initially opened in a reader. Unless otherwise noted, the allowed content values are 'true' and 'false', and the default, if no `<meta>` with that name value is present, is 'false'.

- 'pagemode' : What is displayed when the document is opened. Must be 'UseNone', 'UseOutlines', 'UseThumbs', 'FullScreen' or 'UseOC'. When the outline exists, the default is 'UseOutlines'.
- 'pagelayout' : Page layout when the document is opened. Must be 'SinglePage', 'OneColumn', 'TwoColumnLeft', 'TwoColumnRight', 'TwoPageLeft' or 'TwoPageRight'. The default is 'SinglePage'.
- 'hidetoolbar' : Whether to hide the toolbar when the document is opened.
- 'hidemenubar' : Whether to hide the menu bar when the document is opened.
- 'hidewindowui' : Whether to hide user interface (UI) elements such as a scroll bar when the document is opened.
- 'fitwindow' : Whether, when the document is opened, to change the size of the document window to fit the page size.
- 'centerwindow' : Whether to position the document's window in the center of the screen when the document is opened.

19

- 'displaydoctitle' : Whether the window's title bar should display the document title.
- 'openaction' : Either the destination within the document at which the document is to be opened or a JavaScript program to execute when the document is opened.

PDF Bookmarks 🗒

PDF bookmarks can be created. The bookmark properties defined by CSS 3 are 'bookmark-level', 'bookmark-label', and 'bookmark-state'. AH Formatter defines additional properties for controlling the appearance of a bookmark label.

∨ 🔖 **Introduction to CSS for Paged Media**

   🔖 Contents

  > 🔖 Introduction

  > 🔖 1. Screen and Paged Media

  > 🔖 2. Box Layout

  > 🔖 3. Background Decoration

Screenshot of part of the bookmarks for this document

```
/* Bookmarks */
h1 { bookmark-level: 1;
     -ah-outline-font-weight: bold;
     -ah-outline-color: rgb(0, 61, 25);
}
h2 { bookmark-level: 2; bookmark-state: closed; }
h3 { bookmark-level: 3; bookmark-state: closed; }
h4 { bookmark-level: 4; bookmark-state: closed; }
h5,h6 { bookmark-level: none; }
```

Bookmark level : 'bookmark-level' 🗒

■ Initial value: 'none' ■ Applies to: all elements ■ Inherited: no

Sets the bookmark level.

- 'none' : No bookmark is generated.
- <integer> : Bookmark level. The highest bookmark level is 1 (similarly to the <h1> as the highest heading level in HTML). A negative or zero value is invalid.

19

Bookmark label : 'bookmark-label' 📄

◼ Initial value: 'none' ◼ Applies to: all elements ◼ Inherited: no

Sets bookmark label. When the bookmark label is 'none', the text content of the element is used as the bookmark label.

- 'none' : No bookmark is generated.
- <content-list> : A content list as defined for the 'string-set' property (see Variable strings : 'string-set' (page 40)). The value of <content-list> becomes the text content of the bookmark label.

Bookmark state : 'bookmark-state' 📄

◼ Initial value: 'open' ◼ Applies to: block elements ◼ Inherited: no

Bookmarks are specified as either 'open' or 'closed'. If `bookmark-state: closed;`, the bookmark is closed.

Bookmark color : '-ah-outline-color' 🔷

◼ Initial value: 'transparent' ◼ Applies to: block elements ◼ Inherited: no

Specifies the color of the bookmark label. See 17. COLOR (page 135) for details. No color information is included in the PDF when the value is 'transparent'.

Bookmark style : '-ah-outline-font-style' 🔷

◼ Initial value: 'normal' ◼ Applies to: block elements ◼ Inherited: no

Bookmark label font style is specified as either 'normal' or 'italic'.

Bookmark weight : '-ah-outline-font-weight' 🔷

◼ Initial value: 'normal' ◼ Applies to: block elements ◼ Inherited: no

Bookmark label font weight is specified as either 'normal' or 'bold'.

19

REFERENCES

AH Formatter currently implements the following related specifications:

- **[CSS 2.1] Cascading Style Sheets Level 2 Revision 1 (CSS 2.1)**
  W3C Recommendation 07 June 2011 https://www.w3.org/TR/2011/REC-CSS2-20110607/
- **[CSS3-Background] CSS Backgrounds and Borders Module Level 3**
  W3C Recommendation 17 October 2017 https://www.w3.org/TR/2017/CR-css-backgrounds-3-20171017/
- **[CSS3-Box] CSS basic box model**
  W3C Working Draft 9 August 2007 https://www.w3.org/TR/2007/WD-css3-box-20070809/
- **[CSS3-Break] CSS Fragmentation Module Level 3**
  W3C Candidate Recommendation 9 February 2017 https://www.w3.org/TR/2017/CR-css-break-3-20170209/
- **[CSS3-Color] CSS Color Module Level 3**
  W3C Proposed Recommendation 15 March 2018 https://www.w3.org/TR/2018/PR-css-color-3-20180315/
- **[CSS3-Content] CSS Generated Content Module Level 3**
  W3C Working Draft 2 June 2016 https://www.w3.org/TR/2016/WD-css-content-3-20160602/
- **[CSS3-CounterStyles] CSS Counter Styles Level 3**
  W3C Candidate Recommendation 14 December 2017 https://www.w3.org/TR/2017/CR-css-counter-styles-3-20171214/
- **[CSS3-Fonts] CSS Fonts Module Level 3**
  W3C Candidate Recommendation 15 March 2018 https://www.w3.org/TR/2018/CR-css-fonts-3-20180315/
- **[CSS3-GCPM] CSS Generated Content for Paged Media Module**
  W3C Working Draft 13 May 2014 https://www.w3.org/TR/2014/WD-css-gcpm-3-20140513/
- **[CSS3-Images] CSS Image Values and Replaced Content Module Level 3**
  W3C Candidate Recommendation 17 April 2012 https://www.w3.org/TR/2012/CR-css3-images-20120417/
- **[CSS3-Line] CSS3 module: line**
  W3C Working Draft 15 May 2002 https://www.w3.org/TR/2002/WD-css3-line-box-20020515/
- **[CSS3-Lists] CSS Lists and Counters Module Level 3**
  W3C Working Draft 20 March 2014 https://www.w3.org/TR/2014/WD-css-lists-3-20140320/
- **[CSS3-Multicol] CSS Multi-column Layout Module Level 1**
  W3C Working Draft 5 October 2017 https://www.w3.org/TR/2017/WD-css-multicol-1-20171005/
- **[CSS3-Namespaces] CSS Namespaces Module Level 3**
  W3C Recommendation 29 September 2011, edited in place 20 March 2014 https://www.w3.org/TR/2014/REC-css-namespaces-3-20140320/

- **[CSS3-Page] CSS Paged Media Module Level 3**
  W3C Working Draft 14 March 2013 https://www.w3.org/TR/2013/WD-css3-page-20130314/
- **[CSS3-Ruby] CSS Ruby Layout Module Level 1**
  W3C Working Draft 5 August 2014 https://www.w3.org/TR/2014/WD-css-ruby-1-20140805/
- **[CSS3-Selectors] Selectors Level 3**
  W3C Candidate Recommendation 30 January 2018 https://www.w3.org/TR/2018/CR-selectors-3-20180130/
- **[CSS3-Text] CSS Text Module Level 3**
  W3C Working Draft 22 August 2017 https://www.w3.org/TR/2017/WD-css-text-3-20170822/
- **[CSS3-TextDecor] CSS Text Decoration Module Level 3**
  W3C Candidate Recommendation 1 August 2013 https://www.w3.org/TR/2013/CR-css-text-decor-3-20130801/
- **[CSS3-Transforms] CSS Transforms Module Level 1**
  W3C Working Draft 30 November 2017 https://www.w3.org/TR/2017/WD-css-transforms-1-20171130/
- **[CSS3-UI] CSS Basic User Interface Module Level 3**
  W3C Proposed Recommendation 14 December 2017 https://www.w3.org/TR/2017/PR-css-ui-3-20171214/
- **[CSS3-Values] CSS Values and Units Module Level 3**
  W3C Candidate Recommendation 29 September 2016 https://www.w3.org/TR/2016/CR-css-values-3-20160929/
- **[CSS3-WritingModes] CSS Writing Modes Module Level 3**
  W3C Candidate Recommendation 7 December 2017 https://www.w3.org/TR/2017/CR-css-writing-modes-3-20171207/
- **CSS Snapshot 2017** W3C Working Group Note https://www.w3.org/TR/css-2017/
- **CSS Writing Modes Level 3** W3C Candidate Recommendation https://www.w3.org/TR/css-writing-modes-3/
- **HTML 5 — A Vocabulary and Associated APIs for HTML and XHTML**
  W3C Recommendation https://www.w3.org/TR/html5/
- **ISO 16684-1:2012, Graphic technology — Extensible metadata platform (XMP) specification — Part 1: Data model, serialization and core properties**
  ISO Standard https://www.iso.org/standard/57421.html
- **Mathematical Markup Language (MathML) Version 3.0 2nd Edition**
  W3C Recommendation http://www.w3.org/TR/MathML/
- **Selectors Level 3** W3C Recommendation https://www.w3.org/TR/css3-selectors/

XSL-FO

AH Formatter can also format using XSL-FO:

- **Extensible Stylesheet Language (XSL) Version 1.1**
  W3C Recommendation https://www.w3.org/TR/xsl/

RESOURCES AND FURTHER READING

Accessibility
- **Matterhorn Protocol**
  https://www.pdfa.org/publication/the-matterhorn-protocol-1-02/
- **PDF File 508 Checklist (WCAG 2.0 Refresh)**
  https://www.hhs.gov/web/section-508/making-files-accessible/checklist/pdf/
- **PDF Techniques for WCAG 2.0**
  https://www.w3.org/TR/2014/NOTE-WCAG20-TECHS-20140408/pdf.html
- **Web Content Accessibility Guidelines (WCAG) 2.1**
  https://www.w3.org/TR/WCAG21/

CSS
- **CSS Indexes**
  W3C Note https://drafts.csswg.org/indexes/
- **CSS Properties Index**
  https://meiert.com/en/indices/css-properties/
- **List of CSS features required for paged media**
  https://www.w3.org/Style/2013/paged-media-tasks
- **Priorities for CSS from the Digital Publishing Interest Group**
  W3C First Public Working Draft http://www.w3.org/TR/dpub-css-priorities/
- **StackOverflow questions tagged [css-paged-media]** https://stackover-
  flow.com/questions/tagged/css-paged-media?sort=newest
- **Table of Specifications**
  https://www.w3.org/Style/CSS/current-work.en.html#roadmap

Fonts
- **STIX Fonts** https://www.stixfonts.org/

I18N
- **International Text Layout and Typography Index**
  W3C Editors Draft https://w3c.github.io/typography/
- **Ethiopic Layout Requirements**
  W3C Editors Draft https://w3c.github.io/elreq/
- **Hebrew Layout Requirements**
  W3C Editors Draft https://w3c.github.io/hlreq/
- **Mongolian Layout Requirements**
  W3C Editors Draft https://w3c.github.io/mlreq/
- **Ready-made Counter Styles**
  W3C Working Group Note http://www.w3.org/TR/predefined-counter-styles/
- **Requirements for Chinese Text Layout**
  https://w3c.github.io/clreq/
- **Requirements for Hangul Text Layout and Typography** W3C Working Draft
  http://www.w3.org/TR/klreq/

- **Requirements for Japanese Text Layout** W3C Working Group Note http://www.w3.org/TR/jlreq/
- **Requirements for Latin Text Layout and Pagination**
  W3C Working Draft https://www.w3.org/TR/dpub-latinreq/
- **Text Layout Requirements for the Arabic Script**
  https://w3c.github.io/alreq/
- **Tibetan Layout Requirements**
  W3C Editors Draft https://w3c.github.io/tlreq/

Reference books
- *The Chicago Manual of Style*, 17th Ed., University of Chigaco Press, 2017
- Microsoft Corporation, *Microsoft Manual of Style*, 4th Ed., Microsoft Press, 2012
- Ritter, R. M., *New Hart's Rules*, Oxford University Press, 2005

Typography and book design
- Bringhurst, Robert, *The Elements of Typographic Style*, 2nd Ed., Hartley & Marks, 1996
- Dowding, Geoffrey, *Finer Points in the Spacing & Arrangement of Type*, Hartley & Marks, 1995
- Haslam, Andrew, *Book Design*, Laurence King Publishing, 2006
- Kane, John, *A Type Primer*, 2nd Ed., Laurence King Publishing, 2011
- McLean, Ruari, *The Thames and Hudson Manual of Typography*, Thames and Hudson, 1980
- Mitchell, Michael, and Wrightman, Susan, *Book Typography, A Designer's Manual*, Libanus Press, 2005
- Mitchell, Michael, and Wrightman, Susan, *Typographic Style Handbook*, MacLeHose Press, 2017
- Pipes, Alan, *Production for Graphic Designers*, 5th Ed., Laurence King Publishing, 2009
- White, Jan V., *Editing by Design*, 3rd Ed., Allworth Press, 2003

Historical background reading
Some of these books are out of print.
- Warde, Beatrice, *Printing Should Be Invisible*, The Marchbanks Press, 1937
- White, Alex, *How to Spec Type*, Watson-Guptill Publications, 1987
- Williamson, Hugh, *Methods of Book Design*, 3rd Ed., Yale University Press, 1983

GLOSSARY

Accessibility   Inclusive practice of making content more accessible to people with disabilities. Accessibility involves a wide range of disabilities, including visual, auditory, physical, speech, cognitive, language, learning, and neurological disabilities. Accessible content is also more usable by older individuals with changing abilities due to aging and will often improve usability for users in general. See https://www.w3.org/TR/WCAG21/.

Anonymous box   A block-level box that does not correspond to an element but which is assumed to exist around text that is mixed with block-level elements in order to fulfill the requirement that a box may contain either only block-level boxes or inline-level boxes. Anonymous boxes may also be generated in a table if the table's elements do not represent all of the boxes defined in the CSS table model.

Bind   Fix together, and usually also enclose, the pages of a book.

Binding   The material used to bind the pages of a book.

Bleed   To print content, typically an image, that extends beyond the trimmed size of the page.

Block container box   A box that either contains only block-level boxes or that establishes an inline formatting context.

Block formatting context   A context in which boxes are laid out vertically, one after the other, beginning at the top of a containing block.

Block-level box   A box that participates in a block formatting context.

Block-level element   An element of the source document that is formatted visually as blocks: the element generates a block-level principal box.

Border area   Area of the border box.

Border box   Box defined by the border edges of a CSS box.

Border edge   An edge between the border area and the margin area.

Box   The rectangular box that is generated for an element in the document-tree. Each box has a content area and optional surrounding padding area, border area, and margin area.

Character   A small logical unit of text. See https://www.w3.org/TR/charmod/#sec-PerceptionsOutro.

Containing block   The rectangular box that contains descendant boxes. A box "establishes" the containing block for its descendants. "A box's containing block" means "the block that contains the box", not the block of the box itself.

Content area   Box that contains the text, image, etc., content that is rendered for an element.

Content box   Box defined by the content edges of a CSS box.

Content edge   An edge between the content area and the padding area. Also referred to as the 'inner edge'.

Content-empty page   A page box whose page area contains no printable content other than backgrounds and/or borders.

Crop marks   Marks that are printed outside the final, trimmed size of the page that indicate the extent of the trimmed page.

Document tree   The tree of elements encoded in the source document.

Extent   Number of pages in a book.

Folio   1. Page number. 2. A single-sided leaf of paper.

Font   A resource containing a visual representation of characters.

Font face   Short for 'typeface'. A set of characters drawn with a particular style and with a common stroke weight, slant, or relative width.

Font family   A group of fonts sharing a common design style.

Foot   Bottom edge of book or of trimmed page.

Footer   Portion at the page, typically at the opposite end from the header, that is set aside for supplementary information such as the page number or document title.

Fore-edge   Outside vertical edge of the page.

Generated page-margin box   A page-margin box for which the computed value of its 'content' property is not 'none'.

Generic font family   A font family that will always result in at least one matched font face. The five generic font family names are 'serif', 'sans-serif', 'cursive', 'fantasy', and 'monospace'.

Gutter   Margin at the inner edge of the page.

Head   Top edge of book or of trimmed page.

Header   Portion at the page head that is set aside for supplementary information such as the page number or document title.

Inline formatting context   A context in which boxes are laid out horizontally, one after the other, beginning at the top of a containing block.

Inline-level element   An element of the source document that does not form a new block of content.

Inner   Closer to the spine.

Inner edge   See Content edge.

Intrinsic dimensions   Intrinsic width and intrinsic height and/or intrinsic width:height ratio of a graphic that is specified in the graphic file itself. Not all graphic file formats include intrinsic dimensions, and for some file formats, it is optional.

Leaf   Sheet of paper.

Line box   The rectangular area that contains the boxes that form a line.

Margin area   Area of the margin box.

Margin box   Box defined by the margin edges of a CSS box.

Margin edge   An outer edge of the box margin. Also referred to as the 'outer edge'.

Marker   Bullet, image, counter value, or symbol identifying a list item. CSS2 defines a 'marker box' for the visual indication that an element is a list item. CSS3 defines the '::marker' pseudo-element that is generated by a list item to represent the item's marker.

MathML   Markup language for describing mathematical notation and capturing both its structure and content. See http://www.w3.org/TR/MathML/.

Measure   Width of a block of text.

Opening   See Spread.

Option Setting File   An XML file that describes the configuration for AH Formatter. A complete or subsetted Option Setting File may be provided to AH Formatter to override the built-in defaults. The AH Formatter GUI may also output a copy of its current Option Setting File settings. See https://www.antennahouse.com/product/ahf66/ahf-optset.html.

Outer   Closer to the fore-edge.

Outer edge   See Margin edge.

Padding area   Area of the padding box.

Padding box   Box defined by the padding edges of a CSS box.

Padding edge   Edge between the padding area and the border area.

Page area   Content area of a page box.

Page box   A specialized CSS box that maps to a rectangular print media surface, such as a page of paper.

Page-margin box   A box within the page margin that can contain generated content.

Page progression   Direction in which the printed pages of a document would be sequenced when laid out side-to-side. For example, English and horizontally-set Japanese typically progress from left to right, whereas Arabic and vertically-set Japanese pages typically progress from right to left.

Principal box   The box that contains descendant boxes and generated content. It is the box involved in any positioning scheme. Some elements may generate additional boxes that are placed relative to the principal box.

Printable area   Area of page sheet that a printer is capable of marking reliably.

Recto   Right-hand page where the page progression is from left to right, and left-hand page where the page progression is from right to left.

Registration   Printing ink in one color in the correct position with respect to ink in other colors.

Registration mark   A symbol that is added on a separation as an aid to ensuring accurate registration between multiple separations.

River   Vertically adjacent white-space on successive lines of text.

Root element   The element in the source document that contains all of the other elements (and text). It is the 'root' of the document tree. For HTML, this is the `<html>` element. For XML, it is the document element.

Ruby   Supplementary small characters indicating pronunciation, meaning, etc. for the character or the block of characters that they annotate.

Running footer   Footer content that is unchanged throughout a chapter or part or the whole of a book.

Running header   Header content that is unchanged throughout a chapter or part or the whole of a book.

Separation   An image of a page, or of multiple pages at once, that shows the tint level of only one of the CMYK colors or of a spot color.

Source document   The document being styled/formatted.

Spine   Inner vertical edge of the page at which the pages are bound.

Spread   Two facing pages. Also referred to as an 'opening'.

SVG   Scalable Vector Graphics. An XML-based language for describing two-dimensional vector and mixed vector/raster graphics that is developed by the W3C.

Text   A sequence of characters.

Trim   Cut the printed media to its final size. Typically, the pages of a book are bound and then the entire book is trimmed as one operation.

Verso   Left-hand page where the page progression is from left to right, and right-hand page where the page progression is from right to left.

XSL   Extensible Stylesheet Language. A standard developed by the W3C. XSL has two parts: XSLT, for transforming XML into other XML; and XSL-FO, an XML vocabulary for styling and formatting. See https://www.w3.org/TR/xsl11/.

XSL-FO   An XML vocabulary for styling and formatting that was developed by the W3C. Arbitrary XML vocabularies are transformed (typically using XSLT) into the standard formatting vocabulary, which is then formatted using an XSL formatter. See https://www.w3.org/TR/xsl11/.

XSLT   XSL Transformations. A language for transforming XML documents into other XML documents. See https://www.w3.org/TR/xslt/all/.

PAGE BOX AND PAGE-MARGIN BOX CSS PROPERTIES

The following table shows the CSS properties that apply to page boxes and to page-margin boxes. AH Formatter implements additional extension properties that are not shown here.

Properties that apply to page-margin boxes may also be set within an '@page' rule. Properties that are either inheritable or are explicitly inherited in a page-margin box by using the 'inherit' keyword will inherit to the page-margin boxes.

Property	Page box	Page-margin box	Property	Page box	Page-margin box
'background-attachment'	yes	yes	'border-left-style'	yes	yes
			'border-left-width'	yes	yes
'background-color'	yes	yes	'border-left'	yes	yes
'background-image'	yes	yes	'border-right-color'	yes	yes
'background-position'	yes	yes	'border-right-style'	yes	yes
			'border-right-width'	yes	yes
'background-repeat'	yes	yes			
'background'	yes	yes	'border-right'	yes	yes
			'border-style'	yes	yes
'border-bottom-color'	yes	yes	'border-top-color'	yes	yes
			'border-top-style'	yes	yes
'border-bottom-style'	yes	yes	'border-top-width'	yes	yes
'border-bottom-width'	yes	yes	'border-top'	yes	yes
			'border-width'	yes	yes
'border-bottom'	yes	yes	'border'	yes	yes
'border-color'	yes	yes	'color'	yes	yes
'border-left-color'	yes	yes	'content'	no	yes

Property	Page box	Page-margin box
'counter-increment'	yes	yes
'counter-reset'	yes	yes
'direction'	yes	yes
'font-family'	yes	yes
'font-size'	yes	yes
'font-style'	yes	yes
'font-variant'	yes	yes
'font-weight'	yes	yes
'font'	yes	yes
'height'	yes	yes
'letter-spacing'	yes	yes
'line-height'	yes	yes
'margin-bottom'	yes	yes
'margin-left'	yes	yes
'margin-right'	yes	yes
'margin-top'	yes	yes
'margin'	yes	yes
'max-height'	yes	yes
'max-width'	yes	yes
'min-height'	yes	yes
'min-width'	yes	yes
'outline-color'	yes	yes

Property	Page box	Page-margin box
'outline-style'	yes	yes
'outline-width'	yes	yes
'outline'	yes	yes
'overflow'	no	yes
'padding-bottom'	yes	yes
'padding-left'	yes	yes
'padding-right'	yes	yes
'padding-top'	yes	yes
'padding'	yes	yes
'quotes'	yes	yes
'size'	yes	no
'text-align'	yes	yes
'text-decoration'	yes	yes
'text-indent'	yes	yes
'text-transform'	yes	yes
'unicode-bidi'	no	yes
'vertical-align'	no	yes
'visibility'	yes	yes
'white-space'	yes	yes
'width'	yes	yes
'word-spacing'	yes	yes
'z-index'	no	yes

UNITS

AH Formatter supports the following units.

Unit	Description
cm	1cm = 96px/2.54
mm	1mm = 1/10th of 1cm
in	1in = 2.54cm = 96px
pt	1pt = 1/72th of 1in
pc	1pc = 1/6th of 1in
px	1px = 1/96th of 1in
em	The computed value of the 'font-size' property of the element on which it is used.
deg	Degrees. There are 360 degrees in a full circle.
grad	Gradians. There are 400 gradians in a full circle.
rad	Radians. There are 2π radians in a full circle.
ex	Unit of the value based on x-height of the font. When the font does not have x-height, a value of 0.5em is used.
jpt	Length unit defined by JIS Z 8305. 1jpt = 0.3514mm.
q	Q (quarter-millimeter). 1q = 0.25mm. (JIS X 4052, JIS Z 8125)
dpi	Dots per inch.
emu	English Metric Unit. 1emu = 1in/914400 = 1cm/360000.
dd	Didot. 1dd = 0.01483in.
cc	Cicero. 1cc = 12dd.
rem	Unit of em in the root element. It cannot be used for the value of the 'font-size' property in the root element.
ch	Unit of the length expressing the width of character 0 (U+0030) to be 1. When the glyph is not in the font, a value of 0.5em is used.

Unit	Description
wch	Unit of the length expressing the width of character U+3000 to be 1. When the glyph is not in the font, a value of 1em is used.
lh	Unit of the length expressing the line-height to be 1. Even if line-height="2" is specified, for example, lh is converted into the absolute value. It cannot be used for the value of the 'line-height' property.
rlh	Unit of lh in the root element. It cannot be used for the value of the 'line-height' property in the root element.
vw	Unit of the width expressing the viewport width as 100. It cannot be used with elements, such as the root element, for which a viewport has not been established.
vh	Unit of the height expressing the viewport height as 100. It cannot be used with elements, such as the root element, for which a viewport has not been established.
vmin	Equal to the smaller of vw or vh. It cannot be used with elements, such as the root element, for which a viewport has not been established.
vmax	Equal to the larger of vw or vh. It cannot be used with elements, such as the root element, for which a viewport has not been established.
pvw	Unit of the width expressing the page width as 100. It cannot be used with elements, such as the root element, for which a viewport has not been established.
pvh	Unit of the height expressing the page height as 100. It cannot be used with elements, such as the root element, for which a viewport has not been established.
pvmin	Equal to the smaller of pvw or pvh. It cannot be used with elements, such as the root element, for which a viewport has not been established.
pvmax	Equal to the larger of pvw or pvh. It cannot be used with elements, such as the root element, for which a viewport has not been established.
gr	Unit to specify spanning columns. It cannot be used with elements, such as the root element, that do not have a reference area.

SELECTORS AND PSEUDO-ELEMENTS

AH Formatter supports the following CSS selectors and pseudo-elements.

Pattern	Represents
*	any element
E	an element of type E
ns|E	an element of type E in namespace 'ns'
E.warning	an E element belonging to the class warning
E#myid	an E element with ID equal to myid.
E F	an F element descendant of an E element
E > F	an F element child of an E element
E + F	an F element immediately preceded by an E element
E ~ F	an F element preceded by an E element
E:not(*s*)	an E element that does not match simple selector *s*
E[foo]	an E element with a 'foo' attribute
E[foo="bar"]	an E element whose 'foo' attribute value is exactly equal to 'bar'
E[foo~="bar"]	an E element whose 'foo' attribute value is a list of white-space-separated values, one of which is exactly equal to 'bar'
E[foo|="en"]	an E element whose 'foo' attribute value is a hyphen-separated list of values beginning with 'en'
E[foo^="bar"]	an E element whose 'foo' attribute value begins exactly with the string 'bar'
E[foo$="bar"]	an E element whose 'foo' attribute value ends exactly with the string 'bar'
E[foo*="bar"]	an E element whose 'foo' attribute value contains the sub-string 'bar'
E:lang(ja)	an element of type E tagged as being written with Japanese characters

Pattern	Represents
E:link	an E element being the source anchor of a hyperlink
E:root	an E element, root of the document
E:empty	an E element that has no children (not even text nodes)
E:nth-child(n)	an E element, the n-th child of its parent
E:nth-last-child(n)	an E element, the n-th child of its parent, counting from the last one
E:first-child	an E element, first child of its parent
E:last-child	an E element, last child of its parent
E:only-child	an E element, only child of its parent
E:nth-of-type(n)	an E element, the n-th sibling of its type
E:nth-last-of-type(n)	an E element, the n-th sibling of its type, counting from the last one
E:first-of-type	an E element, first sibling of its type
E:last-of-type	an E element, last sibling of its type
E:only-of-type	an E element, only sibling of its type
E::first-letter	the first formatted letter of an E element
E::first-line	the first formatted line of an E element
E::before	generated content before an E element
E::after	generated content after an E element
E::marker	marker of an E element that has its 'display' property set to 'list-item'
E::footnote-call	generated content that is left behind in place of an E element that is moved to the footnote area
E::footnote-marker	generated content replacing the '::before' pseudo-element of an E element that is moved to the footnote area
E::sidenote-call ◪	generated content that is left behind in place of an E element that is moved to the sidenote area
E::sidenote-marker ◪	generated content replacing the '::before' pseudo-element of an E element that is moved to the sidenote area

INDEX

Learn More About Antenna House Products

Antenna House Formatter

Format HTML & XML for print and PDF documents

AH Formatter is based on the W3C recommendations for XSL-FO and CSS and has long been recognized as the most powerful and proven standards based formatting software available. AH Formatter has been expanded over the years to support over 70 languages, including the newly supported Indic scripts. Today, AH Formatter is used to produce millions of pages daily of technical, financial, user and a wide variety of other documentation for thousands of customers in over 45 countries.

Antenna House Regression Testing System

Automated system that compares PDFs to catch 100% of the differences

The Antenna House Regression Testing System (AHRTS) is an automated system that features both textual and visual comparisons. Now you get more options in what you want to compare within PDF documents, whether it's text, images, or subtle changes like a pixel shift. Use it to compare virtually any paged PDF output from any software! Available for Windows, Linux, and Mac.

Office Server Document Converter

Transform large volumes of MS Office files to PDF or images without Microsoft or Adobe software required

Office Server Document Converter (OSDC) is a powerful conversion engine used to batch convert Word, Excel, PowerPoint, and images to PDF on a server without relying on Microsoft or Adobe software. OSDC is in production with several large corporations converting an average of over 100+ pages per second and lets you take control with multiple API options: Java, .NET, COM, C/C++, and Command-line. Available for Windows & Linux.

For free trials, contact info@antennahouse.com.
More information can be found at antennahouse.com.

A Data Usability Company
ANTENNA HOUSE